Planning and Designing of Subject Gateways

Rasmita Mohanty
Ranjit Kumar Das

2013

Studium Press (India) Pvt. Ltd.

Planning and Designing of Subject Gateways

ISBN: 978-93-80012-41-4

Published by:

Studium Press (India) Pvt. Ltd.
4735/22, 2nd Floor, Prakash Deep Building
(Near Delhi Medical Association),
Ansari Road, Darya Ganj, New Delhi-110 002
Tel.: + 91-11-43240200-15 (15 lines); Fax: 91-11-43240215
E-mail: studiumpress@gmail.com

Printed at: Salasar Imaging Systems, New Delhi

FOREWORD-I

Knowledge is both the basis and goal of human civilization. Learning and acquisition of new knowledge have defined human existence more than any other factor – evolutionary or environmental. Uniquely, knowledge acquired by each generation is passed to the next, thus making the addition cumulative. Pool of knowledge with the generation in which we live is larger than ever. Systems and mechanisms have evolved consciously or unconsciously over the ages to store the knowledge for its ready use in the benefit of mankind as well as its seamless transfer to the coming generation.

Through the ages libraries have been the dominant institution that has been serving this important social function. Libraries have a long history. The earliest library dates back to 2600 BC. Established in Sumer (modern day Iraq), it archived the clay tablets in cuneiform script. This landmark is symbolically regarded as the end of prehistory and the start of history. Horizon of knowledge always sought to touch new limits due to the insatiable urge among humans to delve into the unknown. As a result it came to be highly differentiated. Libraries responded by having a classification system. Libraries at Nippur, dating back to 1900 BC, evidence one of the earliest examples of such classification system.

As a social institution, libraries have kept pace with the demands of the civilization to retain its relevance. At present we live in an age when information and communication technology (ICT) revolution is sweeping all aspects of our lives. It is playing an important role in all our activities. The revolution has caused the world to shrink into a virtual global village, with communication, interactions and commerce taking place at high speed. Libraries find itself at the threshold of a great change, in order to retain its utility. This research work touches upon one such innovation which will help our libraries keep pace with the time by utilizing ICT tools.

Dr. Achyuta Samanta
Founder, KIIT & KISS
Commission Member, UGC
Executive Council Member, AICTE

FOREWORD-II

I am happy that my good friend Dr Ranjit Kumar Das and Ms Rasmita Mohanty have brought out a good publication on the planning and designing of Subject Gateways. It is based on their rich experience in Knowledge Management & Information Technology and in organizing and running the state of the art libraries.

The creation of Subject Gateway enhances the search capability. It provides a single platform to access information on the Internet, without the need to browse a number of sites

The topics covered are: paradigm shift from print to electronic format; basic framework for planning and designing Subject Gateway; the features of GSDL Software ; the creation Subject Gateway using GSDL; and suggestions for further work.

The book is written in a lucid style and well documented. It will be useful for students pursuing MLIS courses and the working librarians who want to maximize the use of the Internet.

Prof. S. Parthasarathy
Former Director, INSDOC

FOREWORD-III

To the best of my knowledge and belief, this book is the outcome of the investigation carried out by the authors with all sincere efforts and diligence. Hence, I forward and recommend that, this book is an original work of its kind and is worthy for working LIS Professionals and researchers and students.

Date : 01/07/2012
Place: Brahmapur

(Prof. B.K. Choudhury)
MA, MLib., PhD, Diploma (Russian Language) Former Professor & HEAD
P.G. Department of Lib. & Information Science
Sambalpur University
Jyoti Vihar – 768019, Burla, Sambalpur
Odisha (India)

ABOUT AUTHORS

Mrs. Rasmita Mohanty, presently working as Librarian in *Tolani College of Commerce, Mumbai (Re-accredited with A-Grade and permanently affiliated to University of Mumbai)*, Maharashtra. She is also the visiting faculty of P.G. Dept. of Library & Information Science, North Orissa University, Baripada and Academic Counsellor of IGNOU. She is a Library & Information Science Graduate with Honours and holds Masters Degree in Library & Information Science (MLISc.) from Sambalpur University, Odisha, PGDCA and Post Graduate Diploma in Library Automation and Networking (PGDLAN) from University of Hyderabad (Central University). She has been awarded *University Gold Medal* from Sambalpur University, Odisha for the First Rank in MLISc Degree in the year 2006. She has also qualified UGC-NET conducted by University Grants Commission of India in the year 2009 and pursuing her PhD. She is into the Library & Information Science profession since 2006. Within a span of few years she has got the opportunity to work with few institutes of national importance like Indian Institute of Science (IISc.), Bangalore, National Institute of Technology (NIT), Rourkela and KIIT University, Bhubaneswar. She has a wide exposure to the emerging trends and technologies in Library and Information science and services. She is a keen researcher in improving Library Accessibility through ICT. Her area of research interest includes Information Technology, Digital Library, Semantic Web, Information Retrieval & Knowledge organizational Systems. A number of research papers published at national and international level conferences and journals are into her credit. She has also edited an International Conference Proceedings and organized one International Conference on Digital Library and Electronic Information Management and Control. She is a Life Member of ILA & IASLIC

Dr. Ranjit Kumar Das has more than one decade of professional experience in the field of Library & Information Science both as faculty and librarian. Presently working as an Assistant Librarian in IIT Bombay and Dr. Das is the Academic Counsellor of LIS Programme of IGNOU. Dr. Ranjit Kumar Das is a Science Graduate with Chemistry Hons., M.A. in A.I.H.C. & Archaeology, M.L.I.Sc. from Utkal University and PhD in Library & Information Science from Dr. B.R.Ambedkar University, Agra. He was a meritious student and honed many merit scholarships. Prior to joining IIT Bombay he has served as Librarian in Kalinga Institute of Medical Sciences, KIIT University, Bhubaneswar for nearly seven years. His major contribution is information dissemination through latest IT techniques. He has designed the syllabus pattern for LIS Programe of North Orissa University, Sri Ram Chandra Vihar, Baripada. He has also been invited as a visiting faculty for B.L.I.Sc. and M.L.I.Sc. Courses by various Universities in India. His area of interest is IT application into Library and Information services, Information Retrieval System and Library Management. He has served as a Member in the Editorial Board in the proceedings of National Workshop on Digital Library-2008 and as Assistant Editor of the Bulletin of Nephrology, Urology-Transplant Society of SAARC Countries and edited an International Conference Proceedings. Dr. Das has organized ILA National Workshop on Digital Library 2008 and 27th IASLIC All India Conference on "Library/information Users in Digital Era" at KIIT University, Bhubaneswar. He has received Best Staff of the year Award for the year 2009 by KIIT University, Bhubaneswar, Odisha. Dr. Das is a Governing Body Member of IASLIC and Council Member of ILA. Dr. Das is the Life Member of ILA, IASLIC, MLAI, SRCPL & ISC.

PREFACE

The present information society is turbulently moving towards internet era. The Internet is regarded as the biggest store of information of the world. There is a tremendous growth in the number and variety of online information resources available in the Internet today. There is also growing evidence that users are increasingly relying on Internet based information for their day to day tasks and they spend considerable time in finding such information but it is very hard to get the subject specific and relevant resources from the whole mass of divergent resources available on the web. It is, therefore, becoming very important to develop an appropriate mean for organizing and providing quick access to relevant web resources. Subject gateways are developed as a best means to access the subject specific resources without waste in time and need to serve through various websites.

The present research work "Planning and Designing of Subject Gateways" has been designed with the highly acclaimed and most popular multi-platform, multi media and multi lingual Open Source Digital Library Software *i.e.* GSDL. This is a maiden work of its kind and is highly useful in finding various web resources including articles, databases, software, associations, technical resources, and various LIS gateways etc. The basic purpose of this book is to empower the LIS community, the students, teachers, researchers and also those who are interested to get the most relevant, reliable, high quality resources in a single platform without need to browse through a number of sites, thus saving the time with the use of links provided in the project. This enhances and improves the searching capability.

The existing book is divided into seven broad chapters. Chapter-1 primarily deals with the Introduction of the Information Revolution and Paradigm shift of libraries from print to electronic format, concept and need of Subject Gateway, aims and objectives, scope and limitations etc. Chapter-2 explains all about the subject gateways, the historical overview, features, merits, limitations and issues etc. Chapter-3 on the other hand, provides the basic framework for the planning and designing of Subject Gateways. Chapter-4 highlights various LIS Gateways. Chaper-5 exclusively deals with the procurement, installation, running, features of the GSDL Software. Chapter-6 practically describes how the Information Gateway has been created with the use of GSDL Software. And finally, Chapter -7 brings out the observations, suggestions and conclusion by the authors. The present work also includes a glossary of terms, appendix.

Ms. Rasmita Mohanty
Dr. Ranjit Kumar Das

LISTS OF ABBREVIATIONS

ACN	-	Australia's Cultural Network
ADAM	-	Art, Design, Architecture and Media Information Gateway
ALG	-	Australian Library Gateway
ANR	-	Access to Network Resources
ACM	-	Association for computing Management
BIZ/Ed	-	Business Education
BSD	-	Berkely Software Distribution
BUBL	-	Bulletin Board for Libraries
CD-ROM	-	Compact Disk Read Only Memory
CERN	-	European Particle Physics Laboratory, Geneva
CGI	-	Common Gateway Interface
COPAC	-	Consortium of University Research Library's OPAC/Cooperative Online Public Access Catalogue
CUI	-	Command User Interface
DBMS	-	Database Management System
DC	-	Dublin Core
DL	-	Digital Library
DLS	-	Development Library Subset
DNER	-	Distributed National Electronic Resource
DOS	-	Disk Operating System
DRTC	-	Documentation Research and Training Centre
e-Address	-	Electronic Address
e-Articles	-	Electronic Articles
EEVL	-	Edinburgh Engineering Virtual Library
e-Journal	-	Electronic Journal

e-Lib	-	Electronic Library
E-mail	-	Electronic Mail
ERIL	-	Electronic Resources in Libraries
FTP	-	File Transfer Protocol
GLI	-	Greenstone Librarian Interface
GPL	-	General Public License
GSDL	-	Green Stone Digital Library
GUI	-	Graphic User Interface
HTML	-	Hyper Text Markup Language
HTTP	-	Hypertext Transport Protocol
IBM	-	International Business Machine
IIS	-	Internet Information Server
IISc	-	Indian Institute of Science
IIT	-	Indian Institute of Technology
IPL	-	Internet Public Library
JDK	-	Java Development Kit *i.e.* J2SE Development Kit
JISC	-	Joint Information System Committee
JRE	-	Java Run Time Environment
Lii	-	Librarian's Internet Index
LINK	-	Libraries of Network Knowledge
LIS	-	Library and Information Science
MB	-	Megabyte
MPL	-	Mozilla Public License
NCSI	-	National Centre for Science Information
NDC	-	National Data Centre
Nzdl	-	New Zealand digital library
OAI-PMH	-	Open Archive Protocol for Metadata Harvesting
OMNI	-	Organised Access to Medical Networked Information
OPAC	-	Online Public Access Catalogue
OS	-	Operating System
OSS	-	Open Source Software
PC	-	Personal Computer
PDF	-	Portable Document Format
PWS	-	Personal Web Server
RDN	-	Resource Description Network

ROADS	-	Resource Organisation and Discovery for Subject Based
SBIGS	-	Subject Based Information Gateways Services
SIS	-	Society for Information Science/Study
SOSIG	-	Social Science Information Gateway
SQL	-	Structure Query Language
TOC	-	Table of Content
U.K.	-	United Kingdom
URI	-	Uniform Resource Identifier
URL	-	Uniform Resource Locator
vLib	-	Virtual Library
VPN	-	Virtual Private Network
VSAT	-	Very Small Aperture Terminal
WD	-	Web Document
WWW	-	World Wide Web
XML	-	Extended Markup Language

CONTENTS

LISTS OF FIGURES

Chapter-1

INTRODUCTION

1.1 INFORMATION REVOLUTION AND THE LIBRARY

The information era with its electronic facilities have came with many challenges in all the sectors of development. Developmental activities are never ending process. Libraries and information centres are sharing the challenges and risks to partake in this major activities.

A lot of revolutions have taken place day-by-day which changed the society. Renaissance took place to explore the truth of the knowledge. Industrial Revolution had occurred to drive the civilization to use the machineries in developmental activities. Presently, man did a lot for their advancement. People are using information as a developmental catalyst. This era is called as "the era of information revolution". It becomes possible for myriad developments by using information technologies in producing and handling information.

Due to the advent of Information Technology, libraries and information centres are being influenced to adopt the technologies in the field of their activities. The storage and retrieval of information have changed from printed format to electronic format. Electronic or digital formatted information becomes popular for its various positive attributes. Therefore, on the basis of collections, the nomenclature of the libraries are being changed as 'Digital Library', 'Electronic Library', 'Virtual Library', 'Hybrid Library etc. with the digital or electronic collections such as online public Access Catalogue, CD-ROM databases, Electronic Journals and Internet access becomes the essential components of the library. Libraries are no longer only the store house, but are becoming gateways to relevant information world wide. It is important for surviving in the globalisation trends.

Day by day, the society is changing at a turbulent speed. The present society is known as the knowledge society, where information plays the key role. Progress of the society in this era largely depends on the frontline knowledge and information generated by the educationalists, technologists, engineers, scientists and so on. Where, the library plays a pivotal and key role in the dissemination of knowledge and information. In the fast changing scenario of knowledge based society the importance of information is vital and crucial. If it is not disseminated within the least possible time, it becomes redundant. In this rising era, the internet is the most important and useful tool for information access, retrieval and dissemination and thereby bridging the gap of the information needs of the society as a whole, or the individuals.

In today's world, the information transfer through the web plays a significant role in the utilization of resources, information architecture an emerging discipline encompasses the design and maintenance of electronic spaces with an emphasis on access and usability. Due to the rising trends of electronic documents, the use of cyberspace becomes popular. The Internet is treated as the biggest information resource and at the same time regarded as the biggest open library of the world. In this information age, internet assumes an increasing importance in the information retrieval with millions and billions of pages. There is a tremendous growth in the number and variety of information resources available on the internet. There is also growing evidence that, users are increasingly relying on Internet-based information for their day-to-day need and spend considerable time in searching information. Therefore, it is important to develop appropriate means for organising and providing quick access to relevant internet resources. As a solution, to this a number of tools and services has been developed to facilitate the searching and retrieval of information much easier. This service includes search engines, directories and other navigation tools etc. But these searching tools including search engines are hardly incapable of handling vast amount of e-resources in a particular subject area.

Therefore, to successfully resolve these problems different subject domains have tried hard to create different subject gateways for quick control.

1.2 PARADIGM SHIFT OF LIBRARIES FROM PRINT TO ELECTRONIC FORMAT

Library plays a gigantic role in the academic world by providing access to the worldwide information services and resources and can help to stimulate research by providing collections and services widely. Traditionally, the library is a physical place where the collection of items of various formats (books, journals, videos, CD-ROMs etc.) are organised along with the services required to make them available to these user groups. Until, the 1980's and 90's the libraries virtually has a monopoly on the provision of information *(Shivalingaiah & Manjunatha; 2002; p. 50)*. The users were completely dependent on libraries for relevant literature.

1990s are seen as a critical decade when information technology intersects with and becomes drawn into endeavours cutting across domain specific research, education, commercial and social practices (*ibid; p. 80).*

The dramatic changes in information technology resulted in sea changes in libraries and new patterns of scholarly information available on network and instant access to the information cutting down the geographical and time barriers. Information professionals have to switch over to new methods and techniques for handling information. In addition to large quantity of print media, voluminous data are available in electronic format, available online as well as offline. With the emergence of non-print materials and remote access, the concepts of traditional library at one physical place is diminishing. At the turn of the millennium, the encounter with new format, new media, new information and new communication channel, a paradigm shift took place which coupled with a change in civilization led to the implementation and dissemination of new forms of information technology. Thus, we are moving into a digital information society and the digital era has been witnessed a paradigm shift of libraries from print to electronic format.

1.3 GATEWAYS: CONCEPT AND DEFINITION

In simple words the term gateway denotes the entry point to get the desired things. But like different sages have different views, the gateway has also been defined variously by various technocrats as well as scientists.

Moffat describes the establishment of the gateways as "a process of identification, filtering, descriptions, classification and indexing before they are added to the databases, which are freely available via www *(Das; 2001; p 221).*

Thus, it can be said that gateways are the internet based search tools to help people to find resources on the internet, e.g. electronic journals, software, datasets, e-books, mailing lists/discussion groups, and their archives, articles/papers/reports, bibliographies, bibliographical databases, organisational homepage, educational materials, news and resource guides, etc.

Gateway offers linked collections of Internet resource via database of resource description with the following characteristics and features:

- Browsed according to broad classification;
- Searched through index;
- Quality controlled due to the process of human selection.

Therefore, the definitions signifies the meaning of gateways as "the gathering place of discipline specific resources."

1.4 THE NEED FOR GATEWAYS

Library websites are becoming increasingly complex in the form of links and services, profusion of print and electronic format, duplication and the general web resources. When contents become massive the function of library websites needs more restructuring. This complex environment has arisen from various factors:

- Innovative ways of printing information and services such as electronic resources, course specific documents , library help pages and document delivery;
- Complex library searches due to the cross functions and links between the online catalogue, journal aggregator, databases, electronic resources etc.;
- The need to identify and present high quality free information resources on the web and distinguishing those from library licensed materials;
- The increasing expectations of users for interfaces to lead directly, without undue hunting, to the information or service they need;
- Many library websites get congested with ample content, general objectives and duplication of services. It is no longer simple and clear that how to do research or projects with a tool that provides gateways for getting information;
- People are increasingly going to the Internet before they go to the library to manage with limited time and to get more pragmatic and authentic information;
- Librarians are increasingly taking librarianship out of libraries and on to the Internet to keep track with the changing demands of the target group. *(DAS; 2001; p. 221).*

Internet becomes popular for its searching facility. Crawler based full text searching facility is a great achievement of the Internet technology. Full text searching is a blessing, on the other hand this search engine carries a lot of searching results. Mushroom growth of WebPages including multi subjects make the users vulnerable to surf the Internet effectively for relevant resources, thus internet has posed an unmanageable environment. The current situation of Internet may be characterised for which the need for gateways has been arised are summarised under:

- Internet as a whole is not well organised;
- Users do not find what they are searching for and still waste hours of time in looking relevant information are the frequent arguments against internet.
- Huge amount of public information are handled by various search engines in a fairly basic manner;
- Search engines have no inbuilt mechanism for matching retrieval to the age, level or experience of the users or to the purpose of the study;
- Web publishing is often very careless in authenticating sources;
- Accessibility is some times illusory and different file formats and protocols require additional software to read files and to achieve cross-platform performance;
- Ease of technical facilities to copy and paste makes copyright abuse inevitable;
- In spite of attempts to create metadata structures, there is an almost complete absence of effective information control mechanism. *(Raza and Eqbal; 2004; p. 86).*

Although Internet is an unique example of making a successful bridge between people and resources but still it is somewhat lacking in the cost effective manner. Thus gateways are very much essential to improve the effectiveness of internet searching, and will serve as a source of information in specific areas and saves the time of the users.

1.5 SIGNIFICANCE OF THE PROJECT

The increasing diverse and global nature of LIS research mean that many users now a days have to visit several subject services in different countries in order to undertake a reasonably comprehensive search for qualitative internet material. So, as a viable solution to this phenomena, existing project has been undertaken to satisfy the needs of the students of department. Practically, the present work is helpful for:

- The LIS community of the locality to initiate their search and refine relevant results;
- It would save a lot of time and effort of the users in general and students of MLISc. in particular by building an user friendly interface for locally stored databases and resources;
- The gateway will practically work as a pathfinder for those who are going for a search of Internet information web based information in LIS
- Information resources are collected for the project and evaluated by the investigators before adding the same in to the existing collection.

1.6 AIMS AND OBJECTIVES

The versatile development of a particular field of study largely depends on its current stock of information resources. The same theory is applicable to the field of LIS. The domain of LIS is growing day-by-day due to the extensive research and development activities. As a result, more number of resources and literatures are now generated and scattered in various forms. The user community is now heavily reliant on the web resources as the web is now dominating the world of information flow.

Due to the continuous growth of internet, no single publicly funded gateway initiative can fully cover the tasks of identifying, evaluating, cataloguing and organising all the internet resources to support the LIS user community of India. Thus keeping all these aspects in mind, the present work entitled "Planning & Designing of Subject Gateways" has been undertaken with the following aims and objectives.

- The intension of the present project is to design and develop similar types in all subjects related to the needs of the department and scholars specific to their areas of academic pursuits, research and projects;
- To design and develop a virtual gateway for web based information resources in LIS;
- To create a path finder for information searching and retrieval in LIS field;
- To create a local database of scattered information resources using GSDL Open Source Software;
- To find out the feasibility and applicability of such a work;
- To make the searching and retrieval easier by empowering the students and information seekers to convey a richer message through the use of multimedia and hypermedia technologies.

1.7 SCOPE & LIMITATION

1.7.1 Scope

The scope of the study confines to the exploration of web based resources in library and Information Science. The scope of the work extends to

- The varieties of Internet resources on the subject domain of Library and Information science.
- The work confines its scope to the structure and building of a local gateway for LIS resources with possible effort of time and economy.
- The project has been undertaken by using Green Stone Digital Library Software (GSDL) for collection building and navigation as it is an Open Source Software and available free on the web.
- It entails only external links to LIS resources.

1.7.2 Limitations

However, this work includes only the web based resources of the library and information science domain, the limitations set forth for the purpose of the present work are:

Firstly, the coverage of the project is not complete with the paucity of time and economy. This type of limitation may be called as Coverage Limitation.

Secondly, in this work, an information gateway has been created on the basis of an Open Source Software i.e., GSDL, which may have its own limitations. This limitation can be categorised as technological limitation.

Thirdly, only links to the possible documents have been provided instead of document stores and full text due to the shortage of time and effort, this can be said as limitation regarding material selection.

This work has facilitated with only offline access. This is the limitation with regards to accessibility.

Lastly, the present work is only a path finder but not a database.

1.8 SCHEME OF WORK

A scheme is the detailed blue print of research works that have been followed systematically during the research work. Therefore, for the sake of clarity and logical relevance, the entire spectrum of the project has been divided into seven broad chapters.

- *First Chapter* deals with the Introduction.
- *Second Chapter* describes about Subject Gateways;
- *Third Chapter* presents the design and development of Gateways: A Basic Framework;
- *Fourth Chapter* highlights the LIS Subject Gateways;
- *Fifth Chapter* gives an overview of the GSDL, an Open Source Software;
- *Sixth chapter* exclusively deals with "Creation of Information Gateway of LIS web resources using GSDL": A practical approach.
- *The Last Chapter* includes observations, suggestions and conclusion.

1.9 METHODOLOGY

Subject gateways are being the newly emerging concepts and today's buzz word, the authors took all possible interest and efforts to create a proto type project on subject gateways. For effective fulfilment of the project, the authors have attempted all pain to obtain the information on subject gateways physically as well as electronically through Internet.

GSDL software being a versatile software for effective digital collection building, the authors have tried their level best to obtain the information. To get a final shape to learn about the software, the authors personally visited DRTC and NCSI, Bangalore in order to collect literature.

Being experienced with the technical know-how about the operation of GSDL software, the investigator selected a limited number of web based resources on library and Information Science from various possible websites which are freely accessible.

In the third and final stage the LIS resources were down loaded from various sites and uploaded to GSDL software under its appropriate categories so as to create a local gateway to the LIS web resources. This was done by going through the file option of the software. In the next stage, metadata were setup for each files thereby enabling the readers to make the query under any one of the metadata elements. After completion of the total wok it was stored in CD-ROM and made publicly accessible.

1.10 REVIEW OF LITERATURE

A literature review is an account about what has been done to the subject of study or to the related field with the study by accredited scholars and researchers, how it is done and what conclusions were arrived at. It is a comprehensive survey of publications in a specific field of study or related to a particular line of research, usually in the form of a list of references or an in depth review of key words. The literature review may give the researcher an insight into the problems so that he/she may be familiar with the subject.

There is not gainsaying the fact that most of the academic research is originated from the research that has been done earlier. The present study also is not an exception. A brief analysis of related literature found in different books, journals and websites give evidence that the authors are acquainted with what is already known. Again the literature review gives a helping hand in avoiding duplication and gives valuable suggestion for the investigation in the days to come.

So, to prepare this project the following books, journals and websites has been reviewed and consulted.

a. ***Emma Place*** (2001) in his article "International Collaboration on Internet subject gateways" has illustrated the definition and concept of subject gateways.

b. ***Das*** (2001) in "Subject Gateways: The clever way to information" gives an overview of the subject gateways, its historical development, features and lastly the burning issues encompassing it. Also some of the international initiatives related to further research and trend are explored.

c. ***Arora*** (2001) in his article "web based Digital Resources and Services: Trends and Innovations" describes about library websites, web based library services based on digital resources.

d. ***Shivalingaiah and Manjunatha*** (2002) in their article entitled "Digital Libraries in the Networked World" discussed the importance of web resources, the rationale behind the digital libraries, web pages, subject gateways including their brief concepts and features.

e. ***Krishnamurthy*** (2003) in "Subject Gateways to Library and Information Science on the Net: An Experience" explores the initiatives taken by the ISIBC library to design the digital library to enhance the user access as an Electronic Information Gateway. The article summarises gateway and some examples of the electronic library impacts."

f. ***Accanoor*** (2003) in the article entitled " An over view of the Subject Gateway: Material Sciences" has created a web page providing information to not only the internal sources at the central library, IIT, Bombay but also described about subject gateways, some practical aspects for the design of subject gateways. The author also enumerates why gateways, reasons for the development of the study and what is material science.

g. ***Raza & Eqbal*** (2004) in "Subject Gateways: its Need and Development Issues" discusses the concept of subject Gateways in view of the recent developments in Internet based information. It further highlights the need, objectives, characteristics and developments of subject gateways. An attempt has been made to indicate the method of selection of information for quality of research content.

h. ***Law and Dempsey*** (2004) authored a very useful article entitled "A policy content e-Lib and emergence of the subject Gateways" descried the emergence of subject gateways and various policies regarding the creation of subject gateways and selection of materials for subject gateways.

For the present work the authors have also visited and explored various websites as mentioned under.

i. ***Dempsey*** (264024010.pdf) "Experiences and issues based on the emergence of the Resource Discovery Network" enumerates the concept of subject Gateways as well as charts the history and development of the UK's Resource Discovery Network, which begins together under a common business technical and services frameworks a range of subject gateways and other services for academic and research community considers its future relationships to other services and position within the information ecology.

j. ***Koch, Zettergern*** and ***Day*** (DESIRE Handbook.html), Chapter-1 i.e, Browsing structure for subject Gateways) discusses why classification schemes are used in the subject Gateways. What added functionality does the use of subject Classification Schemes add to Internet Gateways. How can Classification Schemes be implemented in a Subject Gateway. Among the number of Classification Schemes, which Classification Schemes to be choosen for a particular Subject Gateway (http://www.1-Browsing structure for subject gateways-DESIRE Information gateways hanbdbook. htm)

k. ***Sonker Kumar*** (2006) IISc Bangalore in his article "Tools for information Retrieval on the Internet" illustrated the need for gateways and the basic features of gateways. (http://www.geocities.com retrieved on 29.04.06.

l. A Report of New Zealand Digital Library enumerates and provides data on Greenstone Digital Library Software and it is illustration procedures as well as the technical aspects of GSDL. http://www.nzdl.org browsed on 11.5.05.

REFERENCES

Das (Pankaj Kumar). Subject Gateways: The Clever way to Information: Caliber, Pune, 15-16 Feb. 2001; p. 221-229.

Raza (MM) and Eqbal (M). Subject Gateways: Its Need & Development Issues. SIS 2004; p. 86-89.

Sivalingaiah (D) and Manjunatha (K). Digital Libraries in the Networked World. *In* Electronic Libraries; P.Sadasivamurthy Festschrift, May 2002; p. 50-85.

Chapter-2

SUBJECT GATEWAYS

2.1 INTRODUCTION

The information era has ushered in proliferation of publications. The growing resources of data, information and knowledge flows out of a vibrant world today. They form a composite web, each supporting the other,in growth and action.

Advances in the information technology makes the information storage and retrieval easier and at the same time, it created a problem of information boom. In the Internet era, as the universe of knowledge is passing through a rapid phase of growth, the focus is on Electronic information. Thus, it is not only acquiring sources of information but providing access to information and sharing also. With the Internet, www and information explosion, identification and extraction of information resources is an essential function of all libraries and information explosion, identification and extraction of information resources is an essential function of all libraries and information centres. The web is now transformed into the jungle of information as the electronic information resources are speedily sprouting and with a wide variety in the form and content and is now scattered in several databases but also in completely different systems, which is not possible for the single users to get access to all the relevant information in their area of study as it takes a lot of time.

To keep pace with these phenomena, there is a need to organise and classify this wide spectrum of information. As a solution to this the concept of Subject Gateways has been emerged.

2.2 SUBJECT GATEWAYS: THE CONCEPT

While analysing the whole concept of subject Gateway, two parts stems from the concepts, *i.e.* Subject and Gateway, both the terms conveys different meaning, as

Subject- The concept of subject is known to all subject implies a specific a branch of study or discipline.

Gateway- Here the concept of gateway is important. Simply speaking, the term gateway means the entry point to get the desired things.

Thus, the subject gateways are regarded as the path-finders. The subject gateways are the guides to get right kind of information from the vast ocean of information resources.

A subject gateway can be defined as a facility that allows easier access to web based resources in a defined subject area.

The simplest types of subject gateways are sets of WebPages containing lists of links to resources. Some gateways index their lists of links and provide a simple search facility. More advanced gateways offer a much enhanced services via a system consisting of a resource database and various indexes, which can be searched and/or browse throughout a web based interface (O'Leary; 2000;WD).

Subject Gateways are also known as subject based information gateways (SBIGS), subject based gateways, subject trees, pathfinders, quality controlled subject gateways etc.

According to Dempsey L, Gardner T and D.Michale, UKOLN, University of Bath, UK), "Subject Gateways are Internet Services which supports systematic resource discovery. They provide links to resources (documents, objects or sites or services) predominantly accessible via the Internet. The service is based on resource description. Browsing access to the resource via a subject structure is an important feature."

According to Emma Place, (ILRT, University of Bistol, UK) "Subject gateways are internet based services to help users to locate high quality information that is available on the Internet. They are typically databases of detailed metadata (or catalogue) records which describes Internet resources and offer a hyperlink to the resources."

Subject Gateways are online service and sites that provides searchable and browsable catalogue of Internet based resources. Subject gateways typically focuses on a related set of academic subject areas. The subject gateway should therefore, encourage the exploitation of publishers materials and will simplify material. Integrated into these subject portals will be the existing and developing subject gateways, which will continue to provide free access to qualitative web resources. Subject gateways are a step in evolutionary process.

A subject gateway is a website that provides searchable and browsable access to online resources focussed around a specific subject. It provides a resources discovery mechanisms for accessing a collection of high quality evaluated resources identified to support research in a particular subject discipline. (Raz and Eqbal; 2004; p. 86).

Therefore, it can be said that, subject gateways have an input of identified, selected, evaluated and accessed subject oriented information resources. A quality input provides a quality input search and it is easy for the user to decide whether the output is capable to match their requirements. These type of search facilities are created, designed and maintained by librarians, information professionals and/or subject experts with the aim of providing access to high quality sources of information, and also contain the full range of subject oriented internet materials which negate the possibility of repetition in the search results.

2.3 SUBJECT GATEWAYS: A HISTORICAL OVERVIEW

The subject gateways emerged in response to the challenges of "resource discovery" in a fast developing Internet Environment in the early and mid 1990s (DAS;2001;p220). Due to the emergence of the network information retrieval systems (Gopher, www, Archie, netfirst etc) and access Protocols (ftp, gopher, telnet, http, etc), innovative information technologies and services emerged.

The Electronic libraries Programme (e-lib) was an initiative of the joint information systems committee (JISC) of the UK Higher Education Funding Councils, following the publication of the Follett Report on Libraries. Its first phase saw the setting up of projects during 1995 in the programmatic areas such as; electronic document and article delivery, digitization (of backruns of journals), on demand publishing, training and awareness and access to network resources (ANR). The subject gateways were funded as part of the ANR area and later on it leads to the funding and establishment of e-Libs subject gateways-SOSIG, EEVL, OMNI, History, ADAM, and Biz/Ed. *(Law and Dempsey; sept. 2004; WD).*

A variety of other initiative was developed in concern with e-lib. These included the funding of an Arts and Humanities Data Service (following a joint British Academy/British Library report and a commissioned study on how such service would operate), the commissioning of work on retrospective conversion needs, and the funding for wider use of the union catalogue of the consortium of university Research Libraries (COPAC). These activities were in turn part of a larger, developing JISC information agenda begins in 1991, which included the setting up of the National Data Centres (Which managed access to licensed bibliographic and other data sets), advisory and communication services, and other shared services. Together, this growing portfolio of activity was a result of a belief is the utility of shared action in the construction of academic information infrastructure. In the same way as the network infrastructure was centrally produced and managed, it was felt that a significant part of shared information resource and supporting services could be managed. In this way, the subject gateways can be seen as continuous with other initiatives which were looking at academic information infrastructure at around this time in other countries, although the particular approach adopted here anticipated developments elsewhere.

The call characterises is the aim of the ANR standards as "to consider funding through the JISC to encourage the development of networking migration tools and the growth of local subject based tool and information services" *(Law and Dempsey; Sept. 2004; WD).*

Work was to be taken forwarded in three ways following some consultations, bids to provide subject services would be invited. This led to the funding and establishment of the e-lib subject gateways. These were:

SOSIG (Social Science Information Gateway) which slightly pre-dated e-lib, and in some ways acted as a model for another gateways.

EEVL (Edinburgh Engineering Virtual Library)

OMNI (Organised Access to Medical Networked Information)

ADAM (Art, Design, Architecture and Media Information Gateway)

Biz/Ed. The ROADS (Resource organisation and Discovery for Subject based Services) Project, which provided systems support for the gateways was also supported. Together with some more content oriented projects these formed the Access to Network Resource stand of e-lib (ANR). It was believed that while the community might afford and sustain a series of services at "Faculty" level, that this would not be true at individual "subject level". The choice of subjects was intended to test this, as well as whether these were discipline specific items.

However, it is worth interesting to note that the subject gateways within the RDN are very much seen as central components of a wider distributed National Electronic Resource, a managed environment for accessing quality assured information resources on the Internet (DNER), which aims to deliver a richer research and learning information infrastructure *(Ariadne.html)*

2.4 RATIONALE BEHIND SUBJECT GATEWAYS

The main rationale *i.e.* reasons for which the need for subject gateways has been arised can be enumerated as:

- Many academic libraries and institutions are currently looking for ways to help their users in discovering high quality information on the web/internet in a quick and effective way;
- Researchers and academicians do not always have the time, inclination skills to surf the Internet for resources that could support their work;
- As Internet publishing and communication is becoming more common place this could disadvantage some researchers, as they will miss valuable information and communication resources; *(Raza & Eqbal; 2004; 86)*
- The emergence of a subject gateway as an Internet service resulted due to the poor performance of search tools in the web. As is widely known, most search engines index only a fraction of total Internet Sources;
- Despite the ongoing development and increasing sophistication of some of the popular search engines. They are still not reliable for finding relevant items quickly;
- Users disinterest to visit the library as they get most materials on their desktops;
- Not willing to go through the print material but may be interested in photo copies of the required material;
- Users expectations to get all materials at the shortest possible time;
- Less patience in searching and browsing through print materials;

- As the Internet now-a-days is a time waster, the subject gateways are required as a time management tool;
- The information revolution has empowered us to work faster, smaller and with greater sophistication than ever before possible, but with the right set of tools or skills, we can quickly become buried in the avalancite of information that was supposed us to proposal us to greater highlights efficiency. *(Sonekar; WD).*

2.5 SUBJECT GATEWAYS: AIMS AND OBJECTIVES

Subject gateways operate in web environment. This means that they must available all the time to end users and users expect reasonable response time when they browse the gateways and predictable performance when they search the databases, the subject gateway catalogues expect reasonable response times as they add resource description to database. The core objectives of subject gateways are:

- The subject gateways can be used to promote the particular subject resource.
- To provide current information about the online subject specific resources
- To provide access to online and CD-ROM based reference source such as database and catalogue
- To provide quality information on the web
- To provide links to number of other sites or documents on the internet. *(Raza and Eqbal; 2004; p. 87)*

2.6 SUBJECT GATEWAYS: BASIC FEATURES

Now-a-days subject gateways are well established feature on the Internet. These are the quality controlled information services that have the following features which can be enumerated as under:

i. An online service that provides links to numerous other sites or documents on the Internet;

ii. Selection of resources in an intellectual process according to published quality and scope;

iii. Intellectually produced content descriptions;

iv. Intellectually constructed browsing structure/ classification;

v. Manually generated bibliographic metadata for the individual resources; *(ibid; p. 86)*

vi. The information to be accessed has a definite purpose and theme, and the theme is usually subject oriented;

vii. These types of facilities are created, designed and maintained by librarians/information professionals and/or subject experts with the aim of providing access to high quality sources of information. *(Choudhry; 2003; p 59)*

viii. Each resource selected is evaluated against explicitly quality selection criteria;

ix. Currency of resources is checked by link checking software (*e.g.* ROADS), databases such as OMNI; *(Das; 2001; p. 223)*

x. Distributed cataloguing, *i.e.* a scattered group of subject specialists contributes to the databases;

xi. Use of open standards to support cooperation with other services, *e.g.* Cross Searching;

xii. The resources in each gateway have all been selected according to pre determined criteria, published at each gateway site as part of a content coverage policy *(www.ula.gov.au)*;

xiii. Subject gateways do not posses content redundant links *(Sonekar; WD)*;

xiv. Provides faster access to web resources.

2.7 SUBJECT GATEWAYS: MERITS AND LIMITATIONS

Every thing in this universe has it's own benefits and drawbacks like two sides of a coin *i.e.*, one side is light bright which is visible to us and the other is dark side. The world's most beautiful thing is moon which has also dark spots on its surface, so how the other phenomena can be an exception to this.

Although subject gateways are the matter of technology, it has its own merits and limitations.

2.7.1. Merits

- Accessibility to quality collections;
- Provision of cross sectional searching links;
- Access to huge and high quality collection and information;
- It facilitates its users to communicate with the experts in a definite subject field;
- It integrates into the existing structure of internet;
- It leads the users into the way of information age;
- Subject gateways provide personalised service;
- It also provides reference service within a list possible time;

- The users can join with different discussion groups ad mailing lists;
- It helps the users to communicate with "non-nerds";
- It brings together the diverse resources to the users;
- It also entails the facility of research, learning, leisure, enrichment at one platform.

2.7.2. Limitations

- There is a strong need of awareness of such among the users about such directories and subject gateways;
- The data contained in the gateways may not be updated regularly though it is the duty and responsibility of the host organisation;
- Institutional commitments are the vital component for the continued development of a subject gateway.

2.8 ISSUES CONCERNING SUBJECT GATEWAYS

Organising and providing access to gateway resources on the web has been a problem area in spite of availability of sophisticated search engines and other software tools and sites. The main problems is to give to access to a collection of high quality resource available on the Internet in the public domain. The key issues occurred at the time of development of subject gateways are:

2.8.1 Selection of Information

The selection of information resources to be included in the subject gateway should be relevant to it's target audience. The information should be scholarly rather then popular and very comprehensive over view of the subject area. The added value is completeness of coverage.

2.8.2 Accuracy

In subject gateway, information provided should be accurate, if not, then it is of less or no use. Accuracy can be judged by evaluating the content reliability, error free.

2.8.3 Authority

The authority of the subject gateway resource depend on the expertise, reputation and status of the creator on the interest.

2.8.4 Business Issue

Subject gateways, mostly depends on the soft money (project/research funding) which is temporary and unpredictable in nature thus creating issues for long term planning, collaboration and service development. Some gateways has commercial partners, some were part of a wide service, and some stand alone, which offers various heterogeneous services directed at consumers., learners, and professional users, thus gateways differs widely in aims, and scope, which is the hindrance in its popularity.

2.8.5 Sustainability

In this age where survival of the fittest is the mantra, subject gateways still lacking a good rapport with the professional or scholarly publishing , or with public service broadcasting, and without their active participation the very purpose of subject gateways will die.

2.8.6 Interoperability

It is the heart of all the issues and the areas where interoperability and standard solution are required, namely, protocols, query languages and record syntaxes, metadata schema, subject classification and cataloguing rules. Without solving these problems it cannot dream of a seamless flow of information in a subject gateway.

2.8.7 Cross Searching

If a system allowed several gateways in the same subject area to be cross searched, then inevitably there would be some duplication of results, as some source would be catalogued by more than one gateway. As different subject gateways are having different collection development policies, so the combined results of a cross search will contain links to resources of a differing minimum "quality" resource description. So again it is somewhat similar situation to what today's search engines are encountered with.

2.8.8 Multilingual Issue

As the Internet has been flourishing outside the English speaking countries, so it is required to take care of metadata properly in a multilingual platforms. Here, character set issue is most important. If all the cataloguers and users make use of multiple languages and character sets, it may run the danger of increasing "false positives", where the same word means different things in different languages.

2.9 CONCLUSIONS

Library websites are becoming increasingly complex. Complexities in the form of links and services, profusion of print and electronic formats, web researches etc. when the content becomes massive the functions of the library websites needs more restructuring This complex environment has arised due to innovative ways of providing information and services such as electronic resources, complex library searchers, due to the cross functions and links between the online catalogue, journal aggregator databases, electronic resources etc. The need to identify and present high quality free information resources on the web; increasing expectations of user for interfaces to lease directly, without undue hunting, for the information. Thus Gateways are needed to improve the effectiveness of Internet Searching and will serve as a source of information in specific areas and saves the time of the users. Users would be benefited from the expertise of librarians and subject specialists across the continent and be directed to high quality Internet resources rather than have to locate, evaluate, filter and organise the resource themselves.

REFERENCES

Das (Pankaj Kumar). Subject Gateways: The Clever way to Information: CALIBER. 2001, Pune, 15-16, Feb.; p 220-224.

Law (Derek) and Dempsey (Lorcan). A Policy Content e-Lib and the Emergence of Subject Gateways. 24th Sept. 2004. Ariadne Issue.25.htm.

M (O Leary).Grading The Library Portals. Online, November, 2000. (http://www.onlineinc.com/online-may/ol 2000/oleary//.html).

Raza (MM) and Eqbal (M). Subject Gateways: It's Need and Development Issues. SIS 2004; p. 85-89.

Sonekar (Kumar). Tools For Information Retrieval on the Internet (sksonker@yahoo.co.in).

http://www.ariadne.ac.uk

http://www.nla-gov.au

http:www.geocities.com

Chapter-3

PLANNING & DESIGNING OF SUBJECT GATEWAYS: A BASIC FRAMEWORK

Introduction
Preliminary Planning
Phasing of the Project
Selection Criteria for Subject Gateways: A Basic Framework
Staff and Skills Required: An Overview
System Requirements: An Overview
Resource Discovery
Browsing Structure for Subject Gateways
The Need for Browsing Structure in Gateways
Use of Classification Scheme in Subject Gateways:
Merits & Limitations
Metadata Schemas for Subject Gateways
Conclusion

3.1 INTRODUCTION

The success of any project lies not only on expensive technology, but rather on sound project planning. As planning is the blue print for the success of all the projects, planning plays a significant role and acts as a framework for starting, implementation and the fruitfulness of any project.

Perhaps, because information gateway projects are relatively new, and the projectors/planners often concentrate on technological aspects, a well thought out plan is essential for long terms feasibility of an information gateway. The planning and designing phase of an information gateway project undergoes a structural process as discussed below.

3.2 PRELIMINARY PLANNING

As with many serious projects, a well thought out plan is essential for long term success of an information gateway project. The best way to plan projects efficiently is with the aid of a formal project plan document. An important section of the project plan is a clearly defined set of aims and objectives. Simply stating what a project aims and objectives is not enough. The objectives must be accompanied by a clear set of deliverables, against which the overall success of meeting the aims and objectives can be measured. The deliverables need to be contextualised with a clear and simple time table to help deliver the project within a suitable time frame *(Sahoo & Rao; 2002; p. 1)*

3.2.1 Setting a Gateway's Objective

Seriously considering setting up a gateway must means that, there must be some aims and objectives. This might be used to establish a service for a specific national user community or perhaps it is to setup a gateway for a University Library.

Each different gateway will have a different set of aims and objectives. If the funding is received from the third party then it is highly likely that there are some contractual aims and objectives that have to met.

In general aims and objectives are wide ranging and rather broad statements that require further classification. A measurable set of scheduled deliverables can help focus the general aims and objectives. Deliverables are an important part if a project plan and are after required as a condition of funding (it allows the funding and supporting organisations to check and evaluate that their funding is being used to achieve the projects aims and objectives.

The deliverables should be SMART *i.e.,*

- Specific
- Measurable
- Achievable
- Relevant
- Time based

Making the deliverables SMART can help every are involved in the project both those involved in the implementation and those involved in the funding of the project (DESIRE Information Gateways Handbook.htm)

3.3 PHASING OF THE PROJECT

Many of the tasks associated with setting up an information gateway are closely related to each other. There is an overlap with some tasks whilst some can only be started once others have been completed (nla.gov.au.html) the key tasks and phases of an information gateway project (http://www.nla.gov.au) might include:

Phase-1: Pre-Project Planning

- Outline planning of a project;
- Securing funding for project;
- Producing outline project time table and plan.

Phase-2: Project Planning and setup

- Drawing up detailed time table and plan;
- Hiring staff and developing skills;
- Developing policy documents (scope & selection criteria);
- Technical Planning.

Phase-3: Technical Implementation

- Technical setup and system testing;
- Training of non-technical staff in system usage.

Phase-4: Catalogue Development

- Cataloguing of resources and catalogue developments;
- Service launch.

Phase-5: Day to day Running

- Ongoing Catalogue Development;
- Collection Management

Generally, all the above phases are sequential and related *i.e.,* Phase-3 can't really be started until phase-2 has been completed etc. The actual launch date of the gateway should often be delayed until there are a certain number of resources in the catalogue. Many gateways have waited until 100-200 resources are available before launching. Although the exact number will be largely depend on the staff effort available to develop the catalogue, and the overall objectives of the gateway, (http://www.nla.gov.au/initiatives/sg/paper1999-07.html)

3.4 SELECTION CRITERIA FOR SUBJECT GATEWAYS: A BASIC FRAMEWORK

Selection is the process which involves careful consideration of a number of factors, all of which will be affect the definition of quality resource for the service (http://www.Ukoln.ac.uk). The key factors in the selections process of an internet subject gateways are generic: the users, information resources, and the service itself. The framework of the list takes all of these factors into account, by suggesting five main types of quality selection criteria (Koch and Zettergren;WD).

Scope Policy: Considering the users

- Information Coverage;
- Access;
- Cataloguing Policy;
- Geographical Issues.

Content Criteria: Evaluating the Information

- Validity;
- Authority and Reputation of Source;
- Substantiveness;
- Accuracy;
- Comprehensiveness;

- Uniqueness;
- Composition and Organisation;
- Currency and adequacy in maintenance.

Form Criteria: Evaluating the medium

- Ease of navigation;
- Provision of user support;
- Use of recognised standards;
- Appropriate use of Technology;
- Aesthetics.

Process Criteria: Evaluating the System

- Information Integrity (work of information provider);
- Site integrity (work of the webmaster/site manager);
- System Integrity (work of the system administration).

Collection Management Policy: Considering Service

- Collection coverage and balance;
- Availability of Internet resources;
- Availability of library resources.

A quality resource will therefore be defined with the specific service and it's users in mind, as well as the nature of the information resources. The quality selection criteria for a specific service can be created by using this frame work. Within each of the five areas the criteria most appropriate for the services should be decided, defined and continually reviewed. The frame work also helps to structure the actual process of selection (2_1 Quality Selection-DESIRE Information Gateway.htm).

3.4.1 Scope Policy

The scope policy of a service states what is and is not to be included in the catalogue. This is broadly defined at the inception of the service for the identified target audience.

In the selection process, the scope of the service will effect the first decision made about the quality of the resources.

The scope criteria are the first filter through which resources pass, and so are the most general criteria. They will tend to involve back and while decision either resource falls within the scope or it does not. The most important thing to consider in choosing the scope criteria for a service will be the aims of the service and the target audience (ibid).

3.4.2 Content Criteria: Evaluating the Information

Those criteria are based on the information content of resources. The content criteria need only be applied to the resources that fall within the scope. This criteria involve an evaluation of the resource itself. The fact that the Internet resources are not so relevant to the criteria in this section, indeed many of these criteria have been used by librarians in the selection of books and traditional resources for many years.

3.4.3 Form Criteria: Evaluating the Medium

The form criteria are based on the presentation and organisation of the information. Some of the criteria would be applicable to paper resources as to Internet resources. Users need to be able to find their way around information objects, however, the evaluation of Internet objects will involve checking electronic forms and so will involve different evaluative process. (Koch & Zettergren).

3.4.4 Process Criteria: Evaluating the System

Process criteria are based on the process that exists to support the resource. Unlike forms and content criteria, these will be closely related to the fact that these are internet resources. The fact that information on the Internet lacks the integrity of a published work raises a number of queries about the quality of a resource over time. The system that lies between information provision and information retrieval contains many variables, and some evaluation of these is needed to discern the quality of the resource.

3.4.5 Collection Management Policy: Considering Service

Collection Management Criteria will take account of the coverage of the current collection, and may cause other criteria to be changed or modified as the collection grows (2_6 Collection Management-DESIRE Information Gateways. html).

3.5 STAFF AND SKILLS REQUIRED: AN OVERVIEW

Information gateway projects have several distinct phases; planning and scoping, technical and information setup, administration and maintenance. Each phase requires different skills and perhaps different staff. A gateway project would be able to call on a large pool of staff, this may be the case in some instances, more often a few key staff will performs the majority of the links with external people being brought in from time to time.

3.5.1 Setting up a Gateway

Depending on the exact technology used, there is going to be relatively large upfront cost in terms of time and unique skills, in the setting up of a gateway. The information management issues will require research and documentation. It is likely that the people involved with this side of the setting up, will continue to play a part in the project, most usually in the building of the resources database and the day to day running of the project.

If the gateway technology is being developed from scratch or using an existing system with significant modification, then significant amounts of technical research and development will be required. Staff with the appropriate technical skills will be essential. Additionally there may be a need for an interface designer, to develop the user front end to the system. These skills will only really be required for a set period and set of tasks. As such they are the ideals skills to bring in from external sources.

A Project manager or supervisor will also be invaluable, to help on the development of the project to time, budget and its original aims and objectives. The project manager should be able to operate on both the subject specialist level and technical level. The project manager should be someone who can understand both areas and manage their different strengths and weaknesses *(1-3-staf & skills required overview-DESIRE Information Gateways.html).*

3.5.2 Running a Gateway

The key staff needed for the running of a gateway are subject specialists who will be involved in the expansion and development of the resources catalogue. The exact number of these will depend on the scope of the gateway.

3.5.3 Resource discovery, Working with Information providers, Distributed cataloguing, Cooperation between gateways

Depending on the technology used to setup and run a gateway, the need for continued technical support and development can vary considerably. Under some circumstances the need for technical support staff effort can be kept very low. However, it is essential for the long terms survival of the gateway that a reasonable amount of staff effort is kept aside for technical support and development. Even the most robust technologies can run into problems. Simple problems can cripple a gateway if the technical staff are not these to fix them (ibid).

3.5.4 Skills and people checklists

Under ideal circumstances an information gateway will be able to draw on the skill of staff with the following job titles. Reality may mean that a few staff cover all these roles.

- Project Manager:
- Subject Specialist
- Information Cataloguers
- Technical Implementation Offices
- Technical support offices
- Web server administrator
- User Interface Designer
- Finance officer
- Publicity and Promotions officer.

N.B: Details of various responsibilities of different staffs and their desired skill sets can be referred from staff & skill required overview.desire information gateways.htm.

When skills are lacking within the core teams, it can often be very effective to bring in experts from outside. These experts could be drawn from within the same organisation or they could be commercial consultants. People involved in the technical implementation, user interface design and publicity and promotion s are often brought in under such circumstances.

3.6 SYSTEM REQUIREMENTS: AN OVERVIEW

Subject gateway services need to be provided in such a way that they are:

- Reliable
- Responsive
- Efficient
- Scalable

3.6.1 Reliable

Reliability refers to make sure that the gateway is always available. A reliable service is one that is available almost all of the time, is secure and does not lose all user's data in the event of disk failure or security breaches (1-4-system requirements overview-DESIRE Information Gateways handbook.html).

Subject Gateways operate in a web environment. This means that they must be available all the time both in terms of the initial cost of establishing the gateway and in terms of ongoing hardware and software support costs. This can be achieved through the use of appropriate:

- Network Connectivity;
- Hardware Configuration (memory, CPU, speed, disk space);

- Operating system software;
- Subject Gateway Database, and associated software;
- Web server software.

3.6.1.1 User Reliable Hardware

A reliable hardware should be used to run subject gateway. This probably means using a familiar hardware. It is better to choose an Intel (PC) hardware.

3.6.1.2 User Reliable Software

It should always be remembered that subject gateways operates in a hostile networked environment and needs to support multiple users, so an operating system that can reliably handle this should be chosen (ibid).

Again, it may be sensible to choose an operating system which is familiar, however, it is worth noting to use UNIX based operating system.

If one has chosen Intel based hardware, using Linux as the operating system is an obvious choice.

Open Source Softwares available on the web can often be extremely good.

As, Subject Gateway Software is likely to be rely on a separate web server, the widely deployed, well maintained and supported and freely available Apache Web Server is a sensible choice.

3.6.2 *Responsive*

A responsive service is one that can be browsed, searched and maintained in a way that does not subject the end user and cataloguer to undue delays.

3.6.3 *Efficient*

An efficient service makes the best use of the available hardware and network resources.

3.6.4 *Scalable*

A scalable service is one that can cope with demands placed on it by growing numbers of end users, increasing database size and new service scenarios.

3.6.5 *Future Proofing*

Software and hardware systems need to be regularly reviewed to measure how far they are meeting business requirements. The Gateway will want to choose software and hardware solutions which provides sufficient to flexibility to accommodate change such products will probably:

- Offer regular upgrades;
- Comply with open standards;
- Respond to customer requests;
- Impose no restrictions which tie you to that product, for example, by ensuring that you have access to proprietary specifications of data structures which may be needed to convert to a new supplier's format.

3.7 RESOURCE DISCOVERY

Subject Gateway should aim to describe the best resources that the Internet has to offer in their field and for their target audience. Resource discovery is labour intensive and efficient strategies can help to minimize the number of resources added to the gateway. To fulfil the objectives, the gateway need to:

- Point the highest quality networked resources currently available;
- Point to new networked resources as they appear;
- Finding high quality resources on the Internet can be a time consuming job which of course, is exactly gateways exist to save the end user some of the time and commitment required to discover and retrieve high quality information on the Internet;
- Locating resources to add to the gateway requires one of the biggest investments of staff time and effort and so it is important to find efficient and effective methods of working at this task;
- Gateway managers need to ensure that systems to support resource discovery are in place;
- Individual Gateway Staff need to develop their own strategies for locating as many high quality resources as efficiently as possible *(2_2 Resource Discovery-DESIRE Information Gateways.handbook.htm)*.

3.7.1 *Resource Discovery Issues for Gateway Managers*

Gateway managers will need to provide the system and strategies to support efficient resource discovery within their team. Resource discovery is labour-intensive and efficient strategies can help to maximise the number of resources added to the gateway.

Some of the suggested systems that managers can put in place to support efficient resource discovery within the team are enumerated as:

- Avoid duplication of effort;
- Find the right people for the job;
- Provide training in resource discovery;

- Setup support systems for resource discovery staff;
- Setup systems to encourage the user community to suggest resources;
- If creating a gateway for an academic audience then it can pay to monitor university web pages. Look for library websites, academic department's websites etc. (ibid).

3.8 BROWSING STRUCTURES FOR SUBJECT GATEWAYS

Subject Gateways typically give access to internet resources by providing both searching and browsing facilities. The browsing functions of gateways in particular are usually dependent upon the adoption of and use of same directory like structure often based on subject classification schemes or thesauri *(www.nla.gov.au.//initiatives/sg/paper1999-07.html).*

There are however, many potential schemes that could be used by gateways. A Gateway therefore, need to choose which particular scheme to use based upon the purpose of the gateway and the requirements of the target user group.

3.9 THE NEED FOR BROWSING STRUCTURES IN GATEWAYS

The subject Gateways offer a browsing structure due to the following reasons and benefits.

- Browsing a directory type structure is user friendly. The structure makes it relatively easy to navigate and is an important help if users are not looking for a specific team;
- Users are typically able to choose categories from a subject hierarchy and to use these to make their way through the service, moving down the individual branches of a subject tree;

- On the other hand, if users want to make index type searches, they must invent or lookup suitable search terms. A browsing structure also gives a lot helpful overview of the scope of a service and how a particular service is organised.

3.10 Use of Classification Schemes in Subject Gateways: Merits & Limitations

3.10.1 *Merit*

The specific merits of using classification schemes for subject gateways have been enlisted below:

- ***Browsing:*** Classified subject list can easily browsed in an online environment. Browsing is particularly helpful for inexperience users or for users not familiar with a subject and its structure and terminology.
- ***Broadening & Narrowing Searches:*** Classification schemes are hierarchical and therefore, can be used to broaden or narrow a search as per needs.

Questions can be limited to individual parts of a collection. Therefore, the number of false hints are reduced. Thus, classifications schemes are used in the subject gateway for improved precision.

- ***Content:*** he use of classification schemes gives content to the search terms used, *e.g.*, the problems of homonyms can be partly overcome.
- ***Potential to permit Multilingual Access to a Collection:*** Use of universal classification schemes can offer multilingual access to the same sources without the necessity to translate the description of a document.
- ***Interoperability:*** The use of an agreed classification schemes could enable improved browsing and subject searching across databases.

- ***Stability:*** An established classification scheme is not usually in danger of obsolescence. Because, the larger schemes are now undergoing continuous revision, although they are normally also formally published in numbered editions.
- ***Availability:*** Many classification schemes are available in a machine readable form.

3.10.2 *Limitations*

In spite of the merits, using of classification schemes in information gateways, however, has some limitations such as:

- ***Division of logical collections of Materials:*** Classification schemes often split up collections of related materials. This can be partly overcome with good cross references or by the placing of documents into several classes.
- ***The illogical subdivision of classes:*** Some popular schemes do not always subdivide classes in a logical manner. This can make them difficult to use for browsing purposes
- ***Delays in assimilating new area of interest:*** Classification Schemes, since they are usually updated through formal process by organised bodies, often reveal difficulty in reading to new areas of study and changing terminology. *(Koch and Zettergaren; WD).*

3.11 METADATA SCHEMAS FOR SUBJECT GATEWAYS

a. Considerations and Applications

Generally formatted metadata schemes are used in subject gateways and provides the value added to resource discovery. *(Lynnec; 2003; p 78)* In creating a quality controlled metadata enabled subject gateway, consideration must be given to three aspects, namely:

- What resource (documents; objects; sites) to include;
- What kinds of metadata schemes to apply in creating records to link the content.

b. Determining Fucus and Context

Determining focus and corresponding context for subject gateways will necessarily influence the subsequent selection of metadata structure and schemas. What is the specific intent of the subject gateway, what particular objects are to be archived in its design and what output are anticipated from it? The scope and coverage, deliminations of the Subject Gateway involve criteria, such as subject or topic, language, geographical location, time period, type of resource, groups or associations, formats of material etc. *(2_3 Metadata Formats-DESIRE Information Gateways.handbook.html)*.

Once these questions have been addressed, criteria for the selection of resources can be determined, and sources for targets for those resources identified.

Koch suggests that, the most frequently occurring models for subject gateways include:

- National Subject Specific (One subject, one country, one language *e.g.* GEM)
- National Cross subject (Multiple subjects; one County; one language *e.g.* Dutchess)
- Global Subject Specific (one-subject; global, one language -*e.g.* EEVL)
- Global Cross Subject (Multiple subjects; global ; one language; *e.g.* ADAM)

- Universal (all Subjects; global; several languages- *e.g.* CORC)

One might add that the proceeding typology o4 neither definitive nor exhaustive, and like.

c. Determining Applicable Metadata Structures

The determination of the scope, coverage and selection criteria driven content of a subject gateway will influence what metadata elements and scholars will be chosen to support identification of and linkages to, targeted resources. In general, the types of structures of metadata that might be required to support a subject gateway modelled after any configuration of selection criteria includes the following.

★ *Administrative Metadata*

★ *Descriptive Metadata*

★ *Analytical Metadata*

★ *Rights Management Metadata*

★ *Technical Metadata*

★ ***Administrative Metadata***

House keeping information about the record itself, its creation, modification, relationship to other records etc.

Examples of elements pertaining to administrative metadata

- Record Number;
- Date of record creation;
- Date of last modification;
- Identification of creator/reviser of record;
- Language of record

- Notes
- Relationship of this record to other

★ ***Descriptive Metadata***

Describes the physical and intellectual properties or content of a digital items or object with such elements as

- Title (also alternative and parallel titles; substitutes; short titles etc.)
- Creator (author, composer; cartographer; artists; etc.)
- Date
- Publisher
- Unique identifiers and dynamic links (URI, URLs etc)
- Summary, descriptive notes, reviews etc.
- Audience level;
- Physical media; format; etc.

★ ***Analytical Metadata***

Analytical metadata deals with information analysing and enhancing access to the resources content. This type of metadata sometimes referred to as "Subject Metadata". The elements of this type of metadata may include:

- Subject headings
- Thesauri
- Subject/topic key words
- Astracts; Table of contents (TOC)
- Classification codes derived from classification systems
- Other elements of local importance, *e.g.* department affiliation; link to other related e-contents, etc.

★ ***Rights Management Metadata***

This metadata provides information regarding to restrictions (legal, financial etc.) on access to, or use of digital items or objects. Such elements as the following may apply.

- Restrictions for use
- Permission statements;
- Subscribe/licensing/pay-per-view-use fees
- Acknowledgements;
- Copyright notice;
- Retention Schedules;
- Quality ratings;
- Use disclaimers.

★ ***Technical Metadata***

Technical Metadata is concerned with particular hardware/software used in converting an item/object to a digital format, or in storing, displaying etc., may require the use of such elements as:

- Digitizing equipment specifications;
- Camera positions;
- Shooting conditions;
- Coding parameters;
- Voice recognition and/or real back hardware and software;
- Optional scanner specifications;
- Image rendering equipments;
- Type of file and conversion software equipments.

3.12 CONCLUSION

The planning an designing of the project highlights the fact that gateway development and maintenance are ongoing activities for which resources and personnel are required in continuing basis. The planning and phase of the subject gateway needs a feasibility study to know the user, their information needs, their mode of use, the number of users, the institutions, projects and such a study would facilitate decision making in relation to the selection of materials, metadata structures and browsing structures etc.

REFERENCES

Howarth (Lynnec). Metadata Schemes for Subject Gateways. World Library & Information Congress. *69th IFLA General Conference and Council*. 2003. 1-9 August; Banglore; p. 78-80.

Koch (Traught), Zettergren (Anns) & Day (Michael). Selection Criteria for Subject Gateway: A Frame work. DESIRE Handbook (http://desire handbook.htm).

Sahoo (Bibhuti Bhusan) and Rao (I K Ravichandra). Planning and Designing of a Digital library. *XX IASLIC National Seminar*. 2002; Patial; p. 1-8.

A National Framework for the Development of Australians Subject Gateways; www.nla.gov.au/initiatives/sg/paper 1999-07.html.

http://www.desire.org.

1-2-preliminary planning-DESIRE Information Gateways.Handbook.html;

1-3 Staff and Skills required overview-DESIRE Information Gateway handbook.html;

1-4 System requirements overview-DESIRE Information Gateway. handbook.html.

http://www.ukoln.ac.uk.

Chapter-4

LIS SUBJECT GATEWAYS: A LIST

BUBL
Infolibrarian.com
LIS Gateway.com
Canadian Library Gateway
Australian Libraries Gateway
WWW Virtual Library
ILL Web
Information City
IPL: Internet Public Library
Lii: Librarian's Internet Index
Library World

4. INTRODUCTION

Subject Gateways have been created to offer organised and categorised access to particular subjects or topics whilst they may produce a more relevant search result, this may not be as extensive as that from a search engine and it may not be as up-to-date. Subject Gateways point to research and reference information that has been reviewed and evaluated by subject specialists. While looking for high quality information sites subject gateways should be used. There are a number of subjects gateways in the field of library and information science important among them are discussed below.

4.1 BUBL (BULLETIN BOARD FOR LIBRARIES) http://www.bubl.ac.uk)

BUBL is one of the best international information system as well as Gateway for Library and information science and also for librarians.

BUBL was created in the year 1990 when it was a part of the Glassgow based project Jupiter. Following a period of time, when it was run on a voluntary basis, since 1994 it has received funding from the joint information systems committee (JISC) of the UK higher education funding councils.

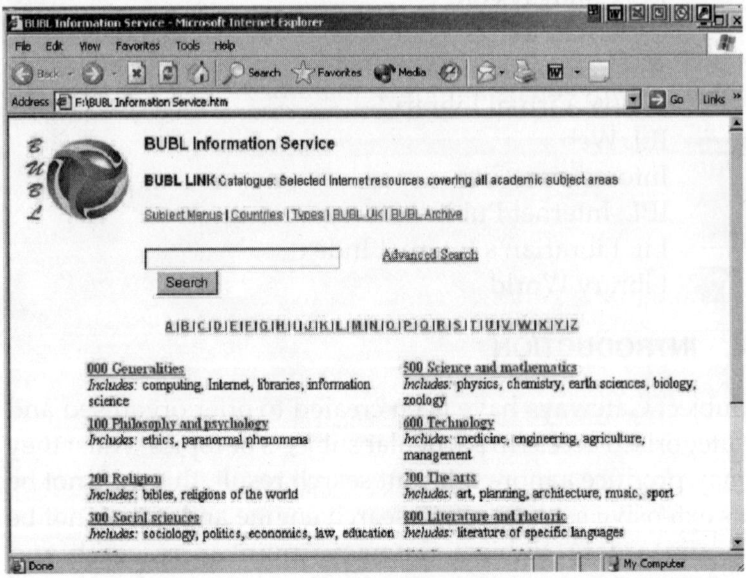

Fig. 1: BUBL Search Page

As a collaborative effort of UK institutions and individual librarians, BUBL provides the best single collection and "the

1st address" in our subject area. BULB's original service was intended to serve as a bulletin board for the academic library community. Indeed, in a review of BUBL Ariadne, Traugott Koch describes it as "the Number one Internet resource for librarians". However, as BUBL was being used by the wider academic community, its scope was expanded to cover other subject areas and it is now been replaced by a new subject based approach called LINK (Libraries of Networked Knowledge). LINK classifies all the resources in the Deway Decimal Classification Systems. BUBL is currently engaged in a project to combine the www and the gopher material into a new www/239.50 service, LINK, extending the BULB subject trees.

4.2 Infolibrarian.com (http://www.infolibrarian.com)

Infolibrarian.com is the most popular Indian gateway site which provides all possible information required by the library professionals in India and abroad.

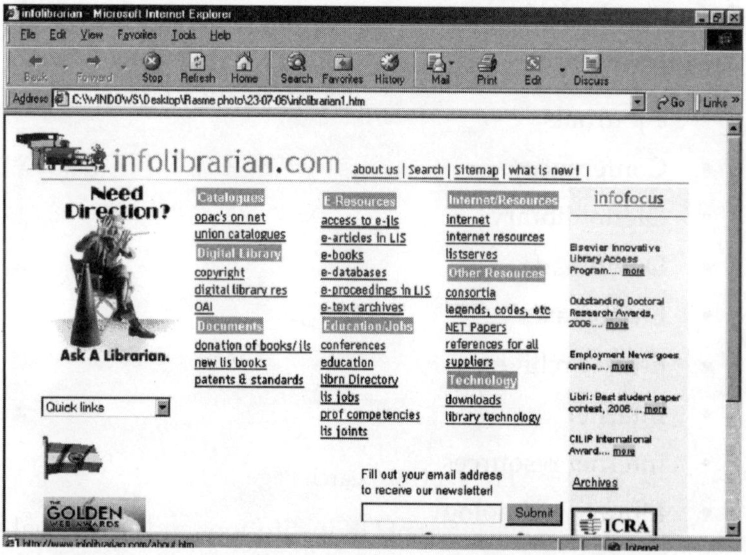

Fig. 2: Home Page of Infolibrarian.com

Here, a group of professionals are working in the area of library and computer fields. The basic motto behind this project is to give maximum information to working library and information science professionals, teachers and students at one place. For this the professionals engaged in the gateway attempts to collect information from different sources and gives brief description, wherever possible.

It provides the following few internet resources, which are very useful in day to day work of our activities.

- Bookshops
- E-articles
- E-journals/Newsletters
- By librarians
- For librarians
- Technical Resources

Selection Include

Access to:

- e-journals
- Conferences
- Digital library
- Downloads
- E-databases
- E-text archives
- Internet
- Internet resources
- Library technology
- LIS jobs

- LIS joints
- Listserves
- Net papers
- OPACs on net
- Patents and standards
- Reference for all
- Supplier

4.3 LIS Gateway.com (http://www.lisgateway.com)

LIS Gateway.com is developed by M.Masoom Raza, who was working as a Lecturer, Department of Lib. & Inf. Science, Aligarh Muslim University, Aligarh as well as the Principal Investigator, UGC Major Research Project in cooperation with Monawwer Eqbal, the Project fellow, UGC Major Research Project, Department of Library & Information Science, Aligarh Mushlim University, Aligarh, India.

The gateway provides searchable and browsable catalogue of Internet based resources related to libraries and information science. It encourages the exploitation of publisher's materials by providing free access to quality web resources.

The data pages establish links mainly to site, which have produced e-journals, e-books, reference, resources etc.

It improves the effectiveness of Internet searching and will serve as a source of information for LIS people. Users would be directed to high quality of Internet resources rather than to have evaluate, filter and organise the resources themselves.

Subject Categories

It provides links to

- Library Associations
- Library Schools
- Library softwares
- Library Networks
- E-journals
- LIS Books
- LIS Thesis
- LIS Resources
- Publishers
- Financial Assistance
- LIS tools
- OPACs
- LIS jobs
- Indian Libraries
- Digital Libraries
- LIS Forums.

4.4 CANADIAN LIBRARY GATEWAY (http:www.collectionscanad.ca)

The Canadian library gateway is created on 15.03.2001. It provides a centralised window to Canadian libraries of all types and sizes. Through this site you can find information and links to:

- Canadian library catalogues and websites

- Directory of Canadian interlibrary loan and changing policies
- Directory of special collections held in Canadian libraries
- Other resources of interest.

Information in the Canadian library gateway is updated regularly. To report new or changed information about Canadian libraries and to comment on any aspect of the Canadian library gateway.

Services provided by Canadian library Gateway

- Search for library information and online catalogues
- Link to National Union catalogues in Canada
- Search for Canadian inter-library-loan information
- Link to directory of special collections of Research value in Canadian Libraries

4.5 AUSTRALIAN LIBRARIES GATEWAY (http://www.nla.gov.au/)

The Australian Library Gateway (ALG) has been developed on behalf of the Australian library community by the national library of Australian and received initial funding as part of Australia's Cultural Network (ACN).

The Australian libraries gateway site has been constructed in accordance with the world wide web consortium web initiatives on web content accessibility guidelines.

The ALG is a free web based directory service which has improved access to information about more than 5,400 Australian libraries, their collections and services since March 1998. It aims to be a directory of current information about every library in Australia a "one-stop-shop" for information about Australian libraries – a tool for world wide users for both library professionals and the general public.

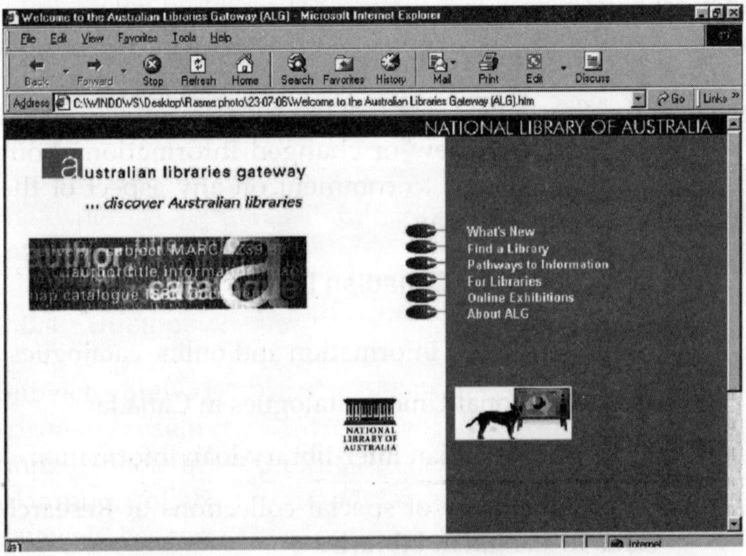

Fig. 3: Home page: Australian Library Gateway

While the Australian libraries Gateway site is hosted by the National library of Australia and staff, they are responsible for maintenance, individual libraries are responsible for maintaining the currency of the information about their own library on the gateway (via online forms and passwords, fax, telephone, email and/or post).

Many resources, such as library catalogues, online exhibitions and image databases, are maintained remotely by libraries around Australia-the Gateway simply links to these resources.

4.6 THE WWW VIRTUAL LIBRARY (http://www.vlib,org)

The www virtual library (VL) is the oldest catalogue of the web started by Tim Berners-Lee, the creator of HTML and of the web itself in 1991 at CERN in Geneva. Unlike commercial catalogues, it is run by a loose confederation of volunteers, who compile pages of key links for particular areas in which they are expert, even through it isn't the biggest index of the web, the VL pages are widely recognised as being amongst the highest quality guides to particular sections of the web.

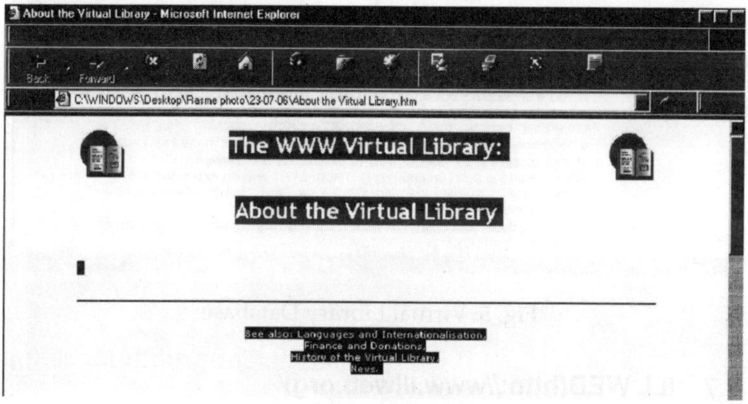

Fig. 4: Home Page: Virtual Library

- The virtual library is a catalogue of the web created by humans for humans.
- It consists of 263 individual catalogues each maintained by its own librarian. Maintainers come from some eighteen different countries around the world and include leading experts from academic, industry and the voluntary secretary.

The virtual library also developed a Databases under the name www.virtuallibrary........Topics Database. This page is skill very much under development. If one wish to carry out a text search of the www virtual library should use the VL search engine.

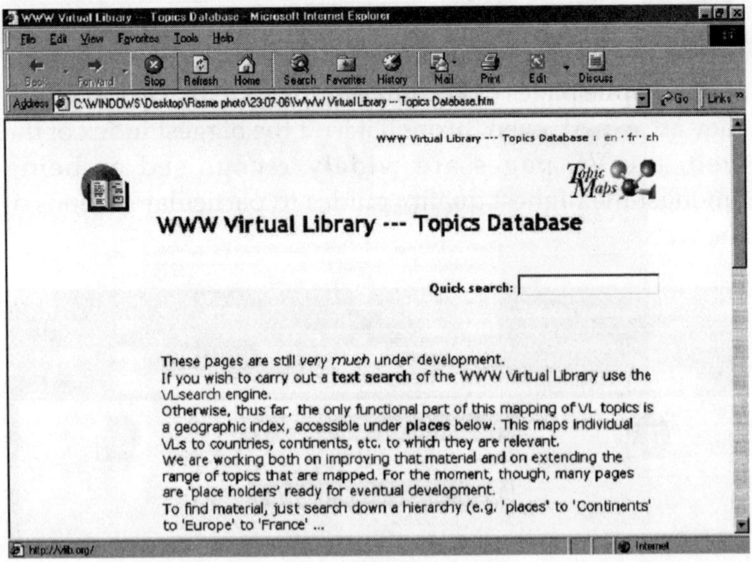

Fig. 5: Virtual Library Database

4.7 ILL WEB(http://www.illweb.org)

ILL web is gateway to electronic and print resources pertaining to all aspects of inter library loan (ILL), document delivery and resource sharing. Designed to be comprehensive and international in scope, IL web features links to resources that will help practitioners to locate materials for their clientele, manage the ILL process, and keep up with developments in the profession.

Services

Finding aids and verification Tools

- It provides links to National libraries
- Library Catalogues and online Directories.
- Verification Tools
- Current Awareness Tools

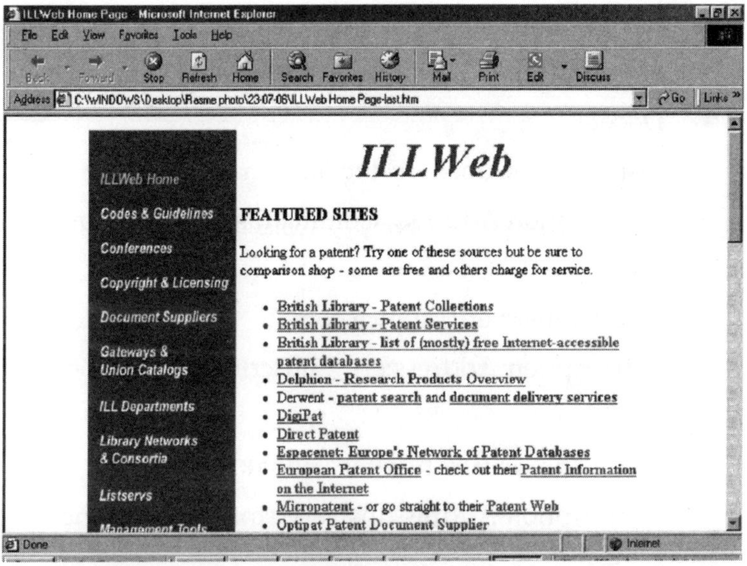

Fig. 6: Home page: ILL Web

- Training Materials
- Projects and current initiatives
- Professional reading
- Listserves

Listserves are great way to keep in touch with your colleagues. Following is a list of email discussion groups pertaining to resource sharing concerns. Some are devoted to a given topic, some are of particular geographic interest (*e.g.* ILL practices in Australia), while others are used by vendors to disseminate product information.

★ ARIEL

- List Address: ariel@listserv.dibsu.edu.
- Subscription Address: listserv@listserv.idbsu.edu.

★ Circplus

- List Address: cirplus@listserv.idbsu.edu.
- Subscription Address: listserv@listserv.idbsu.edu.

★ Docdel

- List Address: docdel@docdel.com
- Subscription Address: Commands@docdel.com

★ ERIL

- List Address: eril@topica.com
- Subscription Address:eril_subscribe@topica.com

★ FISC-L

- List Address: fisc_l@listerv.nodak.edu
- Subscription Address: listserv@infoserv.nlc_bnc.ca

4.8 INFORMATION CITY (http://www.inforamtioncity.com)

Information city is the global online community for LIS professionals. The people who run information city.com are based in London, UK and Stockholm, Sweden. Information City.com have a very long and solid background in the information industry both as user sand suppliers.

Functions Information City

- Helps to build your network of professionals and personal contacts on a global basis;
- Helps you to improve your professional competence and skills;
- Brings you valuable help and advice from fellow professionals
- Keeps you up-to-date with the latest library & information science news and comment.

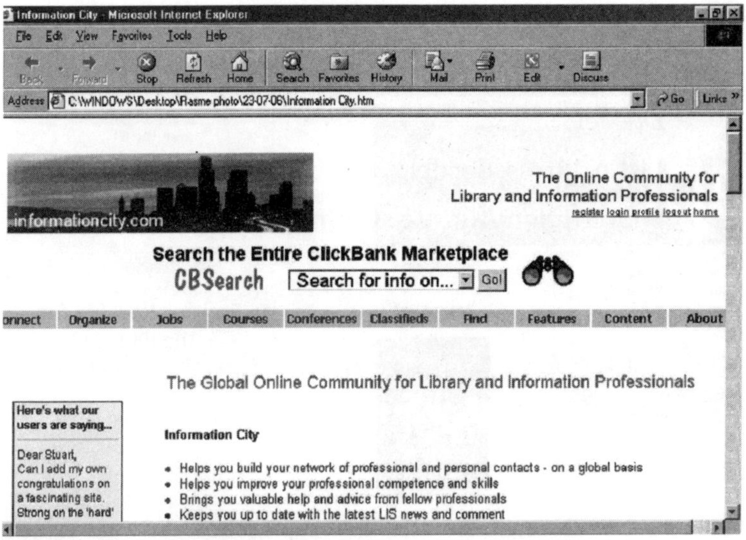

Fig. 7: Main Page : Information City

- Brings you a regular newsletter, which features Lis jobs around the world.
- Provides helpful articles to help you in your job search
- Lets you build your own online community or special interest group
- And even lets you have some FUN

4.9 IPL: Internet Public Library (http://www/ipl.org)

The IPL is the first public library of and for the Internet community. It is an experiment trying to discover and promote the most effective roles and contributions of libraries to the Internet and vice versa. It is a group of highly talented, Creative, Strong willed people working hard.

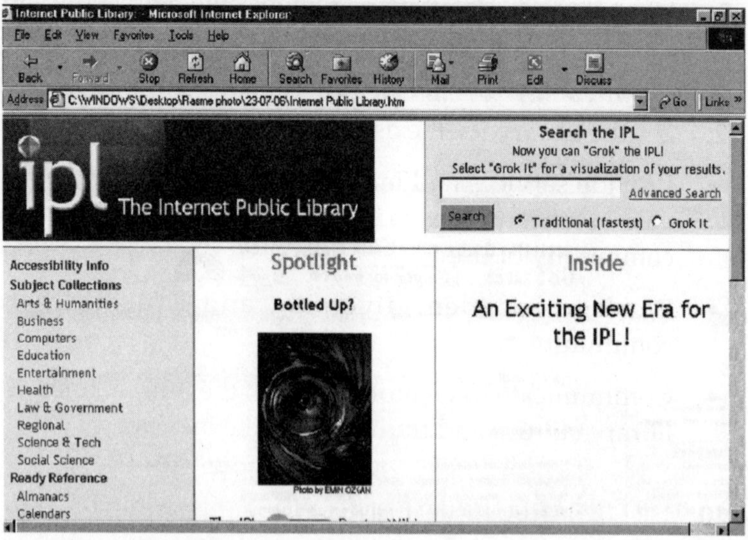

Fig. 8: Homepage: Internet Public Library (IPL)

Origin

The IPL began in a graduate seminar in the school of information and library studies at the university of Michigan in the winter 1995.

Objectives

The IPL project seeks to challenge and redefine the roles and significance of libraries in an increasingly distributed and digital world.

Mission

The IPL has two fold educational mission:

1. 1st and foremost, the planning , development, design and thinking about the library. It serves as an opportunity for its members to learn about user, about

technologies , about management –in-short about all the issues motivated by the translation of the library perspective into a networked environment.

2. 2nd, the library itself exists to :

- Provide services and information which enhance the value of the internet to its ever-expanding and varied community of user.
- Work to broaden, diversity, and educate that community.
- Communicate its creators vision of the unique roles of library culture and traditions on the internet.

4.10 Lii: LIBRARIANS' INTERNET INDEX (http://www.lii.org)

Lii is a publicly funded website and weekly news letter serving California, Washington State, the nation, and the world. It sends out a free news latter every Thursday morning which features dozens of high quality websites carefully selected, describe and organised by its team of librarians.

Lii is a project of the California state library, not a formal organisation, and has no rules, by laws, governing documents or governing officers. They add, organise, publish and maintain websites of interest to Washingtonians. Lii can also provide custom contact services.

Origin

Lii began in the early 1990s as a gopher bookmark file maintained by reference librarian Carole Leita. In October 1994, Lii migrated to a website and was renamed as Berkeley Public Library Index to the Internet.

In March 1997, the Berkeley public library Index to the Internet move to UC Berkeley SUNSITE and was renamed

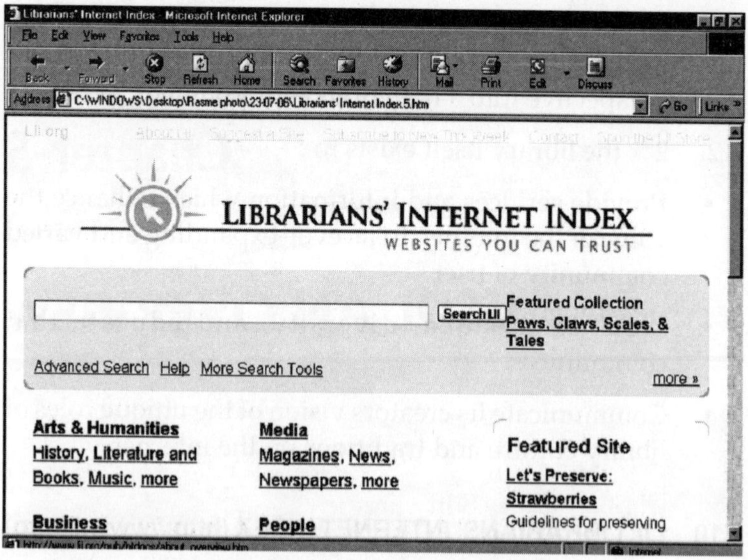

Fig. 9: Librarian Internet Index

the librarian's Index to the Internet (LII). 1997 was also the first year in which LII received funding through the library services and technology Act (LSTA), state funds from the Institutes for Museums and library services distributed in California by the State Librarian.

In the year 2001 the founder Carole Leita retired and Karen & G. Schneider came on board as director.

4.11 LIBRARY WORLD (http://www.libraryworld.co.uk)

This is a gateway designed by library professionals for library professionals. Its aims is to provide library professionals with links to virtually every aspect of librarianship. The site includes a notice board and reference desk, and is reviewed and updated weekly.

Chapter-5

GSDL AN OVERVIEW

Digital Library Software
Open Source Software
Green Stone Digital Library Software (GSDL)
GSDL Used in Digital Libraries: An Overview
Installing Greenstone Digital Library Software
Installation of Greenstone Digital Library Software on Windows Platform
Running Greenstone
Features of GSDL
Conclusion

5.1 DIGITAL LIBRARY SOFTWARE

Digital Library Software refers to the software which is used for building digital collections as a backbone for the digital library. IBM Digital Library and Elsevier's Science server are amongst very few integrated digital library solutions that are commercially available. Now-a-days some open source software are available in Internet.

5.2 OPEN SOURCE SOFTWARE (OSS)

OSS is the software which provides free access to the source code or whose source code is open, thus OSS means any computer software whose source is either in the public domain or mere commonly, is copyrighted by one or more persons distributed under an open source license such a GNU (General Public License) (*Naik; 2005; p. 594*). Such license may require that the source code be distributed along with the software, and the source code is freely modifiable with minor restriction such as to preserve authors name and copyright statement in the code. Hence, it is very helpful for building a customized collection of digital library.

OSS is typically created and maintained by developers crossing institutional and national boundaries, collaborating by using Internet based communication and development tools. Products are typically a certain kind of "free" often through a license that specifies that application and source code are free to use, modify and redistribute as long as uses, modifications and distributions are similarly licensed. Some open source software for digital libraries are Greenstone, harvest, CD Sware, Dienst, Cheshirell etc.

5.2.1 Features of OSS

The prime features of OSS, and the mechanism which drive the working of open source projects enable these features as:

i. One of the most important and attractive feature is that, the source code is available;
ii. It is possible to customise a particular software applications according to local needs;
iii. The software can be modified as to fit the local needs, this includes improving it, fixing its bugs, augmenting its functionality and studying its operations; and
iv. The software can be redistributed to other users, who could themselves use it according to their needs.

This redistribution can be done free, or at a charge, not fixed before hand.

5.2.2 OSS Licensing Bodies

i. Berkely Software distribution (BSD)

ii. General Public License (GPL)

iii. Mozilla Public License (MPL)

5.3 GREEN STONE DIGITAL LIBRARY SOFTWARE

Greenstone is a suit of software which has the ability to serve digital library collections and build new collections (http://www.nzdl.org). Greenstone digital library software is an open source system for the construction and presentation of information collections. It builds collections with effective full text searching and metadata based browsing facilities that are attractive and easy to use. Greenstone is produced by the New Zealand Digital Library Project at the University of Waikato, and distributed in corporation with UNESCO and the human Information NGO. It is an Open Source Software, available from http://greenstone.org or http://nzdl, org. under the terms of the GNU General Public License. It provides a new way of organising information and publishing it on the Internet or on CD-ROM. The aims of the software is to empower users, particularly in Universities, libraries and other public service, institutions, to build their own digital libraries. The latest version of the software is Green stone 3 is a complete redesign and reimplementation which retains all the advantages of Greenstone 2, *i.e.* 2.61 (the current version released on June, 2005).

Greenstone has an interface that makes it easy for people to create their own library collections. Collections may be built and served locally from the user's own webserver, or (given appropriate permissions) remotely on a shared digital library host. Collections can contain text, pictures, audio and video. Non-textual material is either linked into the textual documents or accompanied by textual descriptions (such as figure captions) to allow full-text searching and browsing. It uses Unicode so collections can build any language.

In most collections, descriptive data such as author, title, date, keywords, and so on, is associated with each document. Users can browse interactively around lists, and hierarchical, that is generated from the metadata that is associated with each document in the collection.

5.4 GSDL USED IN DIGITAL LIBRARIES: AN OVERVIEW

GSDL is most popular Open Source Digital Library software, which is widely used to build digital library because of its compatibility, multimedia, multilingual and applicability features. That is why, information professionals around the globe rely on the aforementioned software to build up Digital collections and digital library. A list of digital libraries that have been using GSDL Software are given below:

i. New Zealand Digital Library Project (http://www.nzdl.org)

   A demonstration site setup by the developers of greenstone, the New Zealand Digital Library Project. This site contains many collections, ranging from humanitarian information to computer science technical reports to demonstration collection of Chinese and Arabic documents.

ii. Russian greenstone library (http://gov.mari.ru//gsdl/cgi/lib)

   This greenstone site contains several collection in the Russian language. This site was setup by a regional government department in the Mari El Republic of Russian Federation

iii. Project Gutenberg (http://public. ibiblio.org/gsdl/cgi-bin/library.cgi)

This is an ongoing project to produce and distribute free electronic editions of literature, project Gutenberg now contains more than 3,700 titles from Shakespheres to Dickens to the Bronte Sisters. This site is maintained by ibiblio, one of the original Gutenberg mirror sites, uses Greenstone to make the entire Gutenberg collections available in a fully searchable form.

iv. University of Applied Sciences Stuttgort (http://diana.lok.hdm.stuttgart.de/digbib/gsdl/cgi.bin/library)

Hochschule der medien-an "Information and media" digital library created by the University of Applied Science, Stuttgart, Germany.

v. Grresham college archive: (http://www.gresham.au.uk/greenstone/frameset.html)

A digital library created at Gresham college; London, England.

vi. Center for the study of digital library (http://botany.is.tamu.edu/gsdl/cgi-bin/library)

Texas ASM University- A digital library research site containing prototypical greenstone collections with an emphasis on digital floras.

vii. Peking university digital library (http://www/lib.pku.edu.ca/cgi-bin/bylw)

Two experimental collections created at pecking university.

viii. Canadian institute for Science and Technology Information (u)

A minor site hosted by the Canadian institute for scientific and technical information. This site contains most of the collections available from the New Zealand digital library site and will be significantly faster for northern-hemisphere users.

ix. Music Infromation retrieval research (http: / / nir.isre. vivi.edu)

It is the virtual home for music information retrieval Research.

x. Photograph ibum: (http: / / thatava .ucr.edu / gsdl-in/ library)

A collection of photograph taken by Gordon Paynter.

xi. Aladin special collection digital library (http: / / www/ aladin.wrlc.org / gsdl)

xii. NCSI demonstration collections (http: / / 144.16.72. 189 / cgi-bin / library-exe)

A collection containing thirty books about bridges, all of which are published between 1811 and 1899. The collection was created at Lehigh Universtiy, Pennsylvania and feature a heavily customized user interface.

5.5 INSTALLING GREENSTONE DIGITAL LIBRARY SOFTWARE

5.5.1 Hardware Requirement

- 50 MB for a binary installation
- 155 MB for compiling Greenstone from source code
- 200 MB for optional Greenstone demonstration collection

- 5 MB for documentation
- 24 MB for Greenstone's "CD exporting" function (written and boddie; 2004; p. 1-3.

5.5.2 Software required

- Java Run-time Environment (JRE) version 1.4 or above (Install JRE before Installing GSDL) –JRE is required for GLI.
- Web server (Apache recommended for Web library) (install the web-server before installing GSDL) (apache-2.0.53-win32-x86-no-ssi)
- PERL (Active perl-5.8.6.811-Mswin 32-x86-12208) gets installed automatically.
- C++ compiler, if one wish to compile the source code (visual studio or GCCC)
- J2SE Development Kit (j2sdk-1-_4_2_07_windows-i586-p)
- A web browser (internet explorer 4 and above or Netscape 4.5 and above (ibid).

1. Greenstone Digital Library Software (gsdl-2.53a-win32)

5.5.3 Installation of Perl

Perl is a programming language. As the Greenstone Digital Library Software uses Perl programs, Perl compiler should be loaded. Fortunately, you do not have to know Perl at all. You only have to make Perl available for the Digital Library Software *i.e.* you have to install Perl.

- **Step-1:** To load Perl, in windows Explorer right click on the file named.

Active Perl-5.8.6.811-MSWin32-x86-122208 and follow the instructions on the screens. The latest version of Perl can be downloaded from http://www.activestate.com.

- **Step-2:** Make sure C:/Perl/bin directory is in the path to set path in Win 9x/Me, open the "autoexec.bat" file in the root directory, add "c:/Perl/bin" to the existing directory path or simply add the following line as the last line in autoexec.bat file.
- PATH=%PATH%;C;/Perl/bin.
- Do not forget to reboot the system to affect the changes to the path.
- In case of NT/2000/XP, go to control panel- system, you will see the following screen.

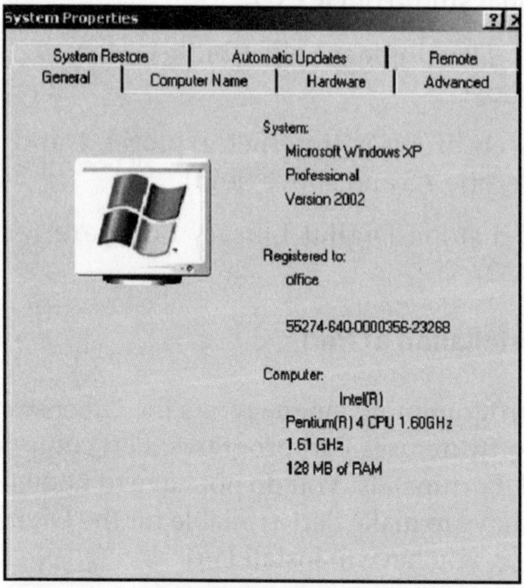

Fig. 10: Systems Properties Window

In the above screen choose advance and you will see the following screen.

In the above scree under "system variables" add C:/Perl/bin to the existing path. Press OK and REBOOT the system to affect the changes.

5.5.3.1 Java Installation

The J2SE Development Kit (JDK) can be loaded from the site http://dlc.sun.com/jdk/j2sdk-1_4_2_07-windows-i586-p.exe. The above software delivers J2SE in the forms of J2SE Development Kit (JDK) and an associated Java Runtime Environment (JRE). To install the Java Development kit please download the software from the above mentioned site and double click the j2sdk_4_2_07-windows-i568-p.exe file. Follow the steps as presented. The JRE is required for running the GLI (Greenstone Librarian Interface), which is essential to build the collections.

5.6 INSTALLATION OF GREENSTONE DIGITAL LIBRARY SOFTWARE ON WINDOWS PLATFORM

5.6.1 Introduction

The Green Stone Digital Software runs on different platforms, and different configurations, as summarised in Figure 1.

Versions of Greenstone are available for both windows and Unix, as binaries and in source code form. The Greenstone user interface uses a web browser: Netscape Navigator or Internet Explorer (version 4.0 or greater in both cases) are both suitable. In case you don't already have a web browser, windows versions of Netscape are provided on the CDROM (witten and Boddie; 2004; p 1-3)

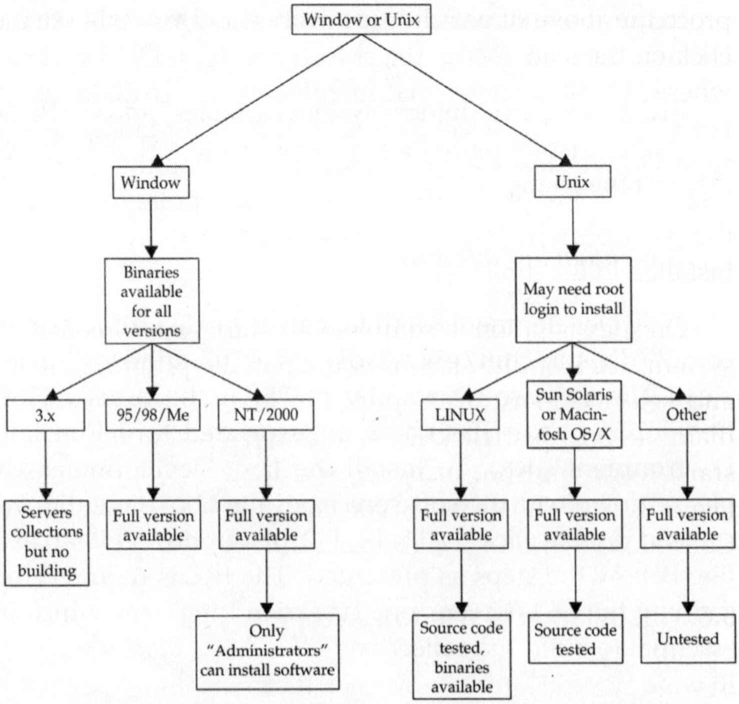

Fig. 11: The different options for windows and UNIX version of Greenstone

5.6.2 Simple Installation

For windows users, it you want just a simple, straight forward installation, go through the following "simple installation" procedure. The Greenstone system occupies about 40 MB of disk space. If you choose any thing other than the default setup, you will have to decide whether you want to install the binary code or the source code. If in doubt, choose the binary code. The installation procedure is the same for both. The following sections tell you more about the options you will be presented with.

To install the windows version from the CD-ROM, insert the disk into the drive (*e.g.* into D:). If the installation procedure does not start automatically after about 20 seconds, click on the start menu, select Run and type D:/setup.exe, where "D" is the letter that identifies you CD-ROM drive. For windows 3.1, select Run from the "File Manager" and type D:/windows/win 3.1/setup.exe. For the simplest installation, just accept the default a t each point by clicking the Next button. That's all you need to do Greenstone is installed in the directory C:/Programs Files/gsdl/

Once installation is complete, to start your Greenstone systems click on the start button, open the program menu, and select Greenstone Digital Library. This brings up a dialogue box: just click Enter Library. This automatically starts your Internet browser and loads the Greenstone Digital Library home page. You enter the Greenstone Demo Collection by clicking on its icon (ibid, p. 8-15)

5.6.3 Installation of Windows Version: Graphic interface

In windows explorer double click the GSDL folder, then the following icon will appear in the screen. To uncompress the software files double click the icon as in the Figure 11.

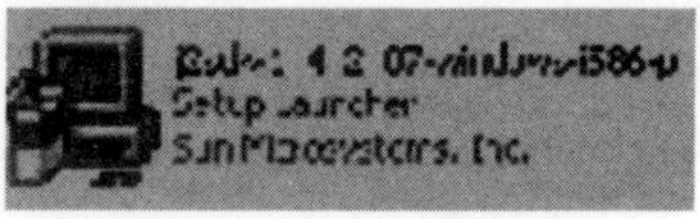

Fig. 12: Setup Icon

Step-2:

It will first ask for the language of the Greenstone digital library software installation wizard like English, French, Russian and Spanish as in the Figure 12, below.

The next step is the License agreement for the GSDL software which comes under the GNU public License. The

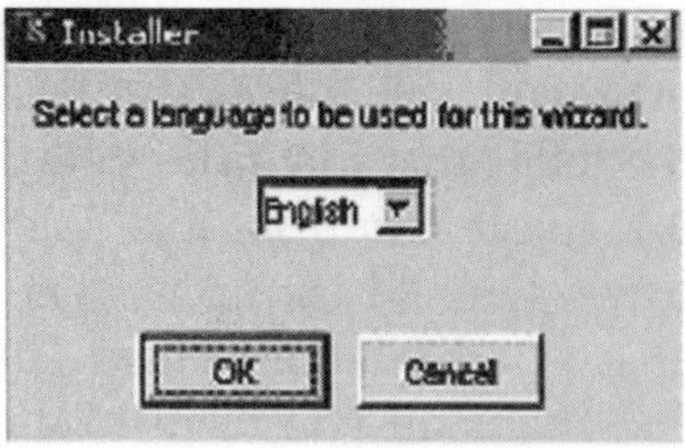

Fig. 13: Installer Language option

following screen appears, displaying the software License Agreement. A few words about GNU General Public License: This is a major trend in the field of IT. Many organisations and individuals are coming forward to offer software free of cost including the source code. This encourages the development of the software by actively participating in the use and also offering programming expertise. LINUX operating system is very good example of this trend, so is Apache web server, Postgre SQL DBMS, the list goes on. Greenstone Digital library software is offered under GPL.

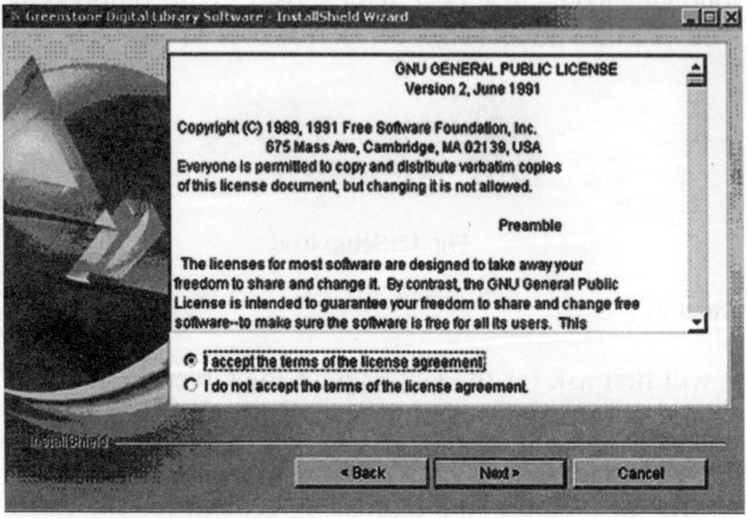

Fig. 14: Software License Agreement

Please read the license completely by using the scroll bar. If you are more interested, visit the site www.gnu.org. click on the 'Accept the term of license agreement' button to move to the next screen.

Step-3:

Once the choice is made in the earlier source, the next screen allows you to choose the directory where the DL software is to be loaded. By default, it takes "C:\program files\greenstone" as the home directory of the DL Software. You can change to another directory by clicking on "Browse" button.

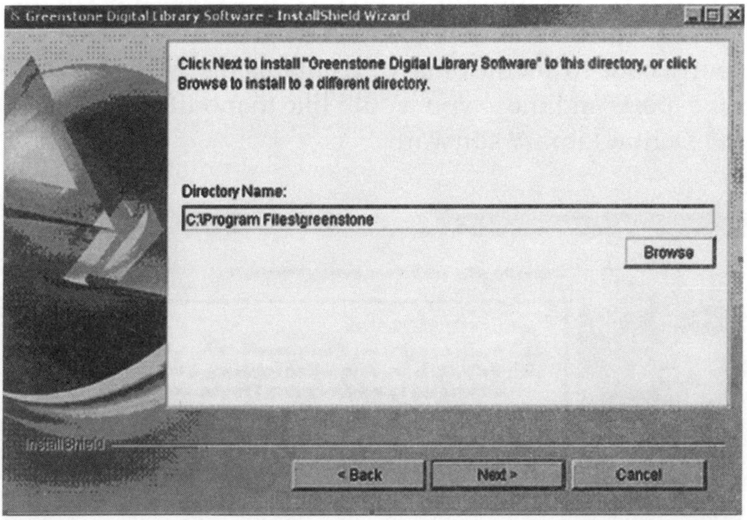

Fig. 15: Path Setting for the Greenstone Installation

Step-4:

In the following screen you will have three choices. If you do not have a web server and do not intend to offer your digital library collection on a network and would like to use it as a stand-alone version, you should choose, "local library". In other words, the digital library works on the system where it is loaded and will not be accessible from other systems on a network.

If you wish to make your digital collection available either on internet or intranet, you should choose "web library". However, in this case you are required to install web server. In case of MS-Windows, it can be either IIS (Internet Information server) or PWS (personal web server). In case of LINUX, it is normally the Apache Web server in case of XP, the IIS is normally loaded at the time of Os installation. In case of win 9x/Me, it should be loaded separately. The option 'source code' loads the Digital Library software source code. You have to compile the source code to get the binary executable files. This is meant for experts and those you would like to modify or improve the Digital Library software.

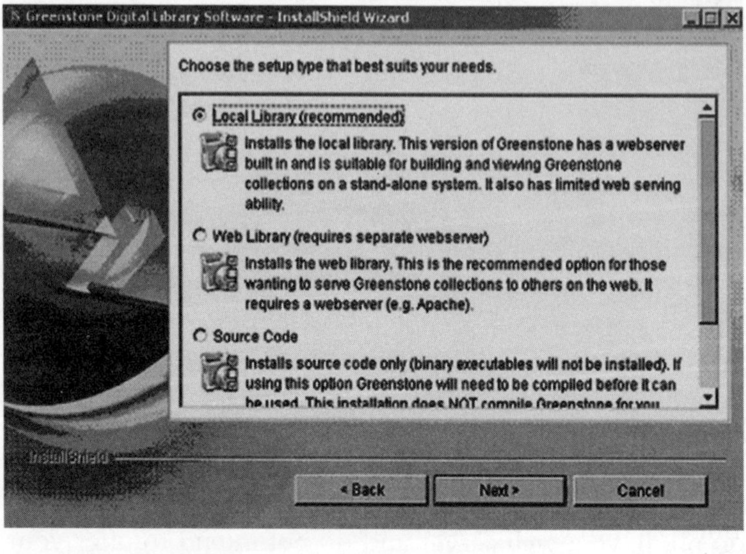

Fig. 16: Greenstone Installation Type

Step-5:

The next screen allows you to set the administrator password. By default, the password is "admin". Definitely, it is a bad idea to choose the default. You should choose another password, so that others can not add or delete files to your Digital Library collections.

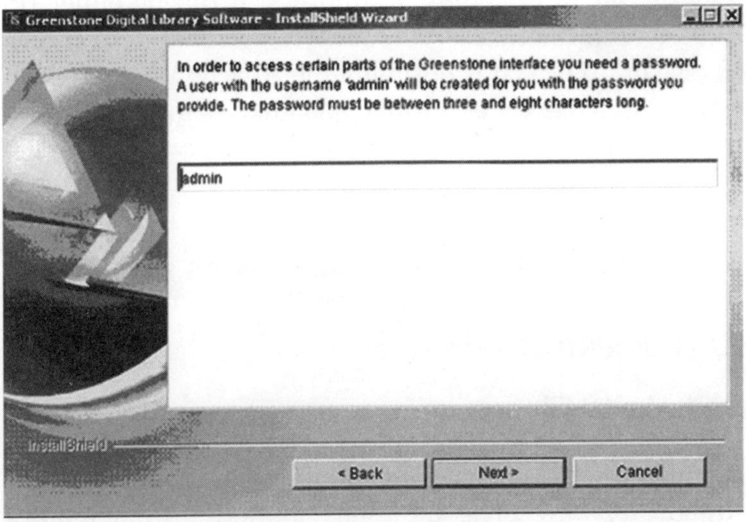

Fig. 17: Password option for GSDL

Step-6:

The next option will ask you to copy the http.conf file of the Apache directory in order to make the digital library accessible to the rest of world, which is meant for the web library.

This is the final step of Installation Process. Just click the finish button in the screen.

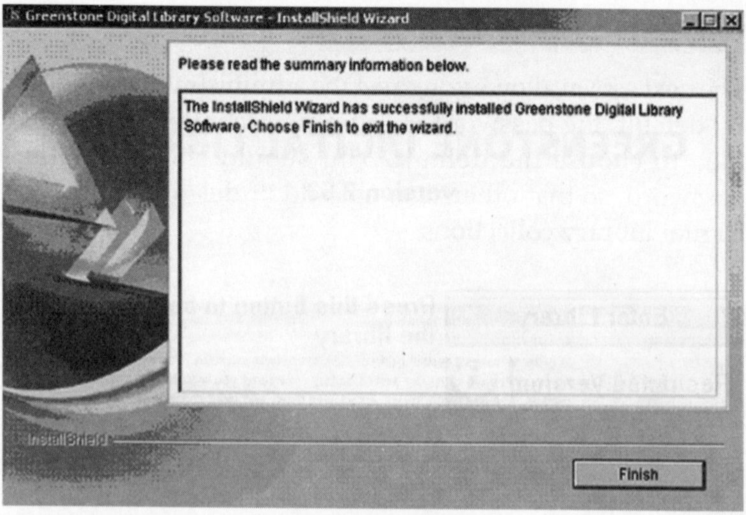

Fig. 18: Displays Finishing of Installing GSDL Software

5.7 RUNNING GREENSTONE

5.7.1 Local Library

Running the Greenstone Digital Library as a local library is straight forward. Press the "start" button of the windows and go to programs, you will see "Green Stone Digital Library" in the menu with a submenu having the items "Readme.txt", "Uninstall Greenstone" and "Greenstone Digital Library". If you choose "Green stone Digital Library" the following screen appear.

In the above screen, you require Netscape Browser Internet Explorer installed to use the "Restricted Version" and is only useful when the software does not work straight away. If there are no problems during the installation, click "Enter Library". The Greenstone software does many required procedures automatically and opens the software in a browser.

Fig. 19: Local Lib.

5.8 FEATURES OF GREEN STONE DIGITAL SOFTWARE

5.8.1 Accessible via web Browser

Collections are accessed through a standard web browser (Netscape or Internet explorer) and combine easy to use browsing with powerful search facilities.

5.8.2 Full text and Field Search

The user can search the full text of the document or choose between indexes built from different part of the documents. For example, some of collections have an index of full documents, an index of sections, an index of titles, and of authors, each of which can be searched for particular words or phrases. Results can be removed by relevance or sorted by a metadata element.

5.8.3 Flexible Browsing Facilities

The user can browse lists of authors, lists of titles, lists of date, classification structure and so on. Different collections may offer different browsing facilities and even within a collection, a broad variety of browsing interface are available. Browsing and searching interfaces are constructed during the building process, according to collection configuration information.

5.8.4 Creates Access Structure Automatically

The Greenstone software creates information collections that are very easy to maintain. All searching and browsing structures are built directly from the document themselves. No link are inserted by hand, but existing links in original are maintained. This means that if new documents in the same format become available, they can be merged into the collection automatically. Indeed for some collections this is done by processes that wake up regularly, scout for new material, and rebuild the indexes all without manual interventions.

5.8.5 Makes use of Available Metadata

Metadata, which is descriptive information such as author, title, date, keywords, and so on, may be associated with each documents, or with individual sections within documents. Metadata is used as the raw material for browsing indexes. The Dublin Core metadata sets used for most electronic documents, however provision is made for other scheme also,

5.8.6 Plug ins Extends the System's Capability

In order to accommodate different kind of source documents the software is organised in such away that "Plug in" can be written for new documents types. Plugin is currently for plain text.HTML, word PDF, Postscript, E-mail, are some proprietary format. A collection may have source documents in different forms. In order to build browsing indexes from metadata, an analogous scheme of "classifiers" is used. Classifiers creates browsing indexes of various kinds based on metadata.

5.8.7 Multi Platform

Collections can be served on windows and UNIX, with an external web server or a built-in-one. It is very easy to install. For the default windows installations absolutely no configuration is necessary, and end users routinely install Greenstone on their personal laptops or workstations. Institutional users run it on their main web server. Where it interoperates with standard web server software (*e.g.* Apache).

5.8.8 Metadata Driven

Browsing indexes are built from metadata. Metadata may be associated with each document or with individual sections within documents. It must be provided explicitly or derivable automatically from the source documents.

5.8.9 Multi Language

Unicode is used throughout and is converted on the-fly-to an encoding supported by the user's web browser. Separate indexes can be built for different language: a plugin allows automatic language identification for multilingual collections.

5.8.10 International

The interface is available in multiple language new ones are easy to add.

5.8.11 Large Scale

Collections containing millions of documents, and up to several gigabytes, have been built. Full text searching is first compression is used to reduce the size of the indexes and text.

5.8.12 Z39.50 Compatible

The z39.50 protocol is supported for accessing external servers and for presenting Greenstone collections to external clients.

5.8.13 Interoperability

Greenstone is highly interoperable using contemporary standards, it incorporates a server that can serve any collection over the OAI-PMH (Open Archives Protocol for metadata Harvesting) and Greenstone can harvest documents over OAI-PMH and include them in a collection.

5.8.14 customization

Greenstone is specifically designed to be highly extensible and customisable. New document and metadata formats are accommodated by writing "pluglins" (in Perl) Analogously, new metadata browsing structures can be implemented by writing "classifiers". The user interface look-and -feel can be altered using "macros" written in a simple macro language. A corba protocol allows agents (*e.g.* in Java) to use all the facilities associated with document collections. Finally, the source code, in C++ and Perl, is available and accessible for modification.

5.8.15 Documentation

Extensive documentation for the Greenstone software is available.

Greenstone Provides

a. ***Flexible searching***

Users can search the documents, full text, choosing between indexes built from different parts. Queries can be ranked or Boolean; terms can be stemmed or unstemmed, case folded or not etc.

b. ***Flexible browsing***

Users can browse lists of authors, lists of titles, list of dates, hierarchical classification structure and so on. Different collection offer different browsing facilities, determined at build time.

c. ***Zero Maintenance***

All structures built directly from the documents themselves. New documents in the same format can be merged into the collection automatically. No links need be inserted by hand, but existing hypertext links in the original documents, leading both within and outside the collection are preserved.

d. ***Phrases and key phrases***

Standard classifiers create phrase and key phrase. Indexes of text or indeed any metadata.

e. ***Sustained operation***

New collections can be installed without bringing the system down. Even user rarely notice when a collection is updated.

f. ***Interfaces***

Greenstone provides two separate interactive interfaces, the Reader interface and the librarian interface. End users access the digital library through the Reader interface, which operates within a web browser.

The librarian interface is a Java based graphical user interface (also available as an applet) that makes it easy to gather material for a collection (down loading it from the web where necessary)

g. Mailing list

There is a mailing list intended primarily for discussion about the Greenstone digital Library software. Active users of Greenstone should consider joining the mailing list and contributing to the discussions. To subscribe, go to https://list.scms.waikato.ac.nz/mailman/listinfo/greenstone-users. To send a message to the list, address it to greenstone users @list.scms,waikato.ac.nz

h. Tutorial Exercise

Greenstone provides a tutorial exercise which teaches its about various aspects of greenstone.

5.9 CONCLUSION

GSDL is fairly comprehensive and easy to use software. It can be used to create digital collections ranging from a small library to a large one. The facility of having a graphical user interface (web browser) and command line interface is very advantageous. Advanced users good at programming can develop a customized collection using the command line. In the content of end users aspect GSDL has both keyword and full text searching option. But GSDL is not completely 100% perfect. It has some drawbacks also. Like, when a web documents collection is built through the web browser interface, it indexes all the hyper linked files also, which makes it very cumbersome for the users to browse through the bulky list of files.

But overall it is a very flexible software. Being an open source software, it can be customized and improved further. Also, its being available free of cost, it is very well suited for small and medium sized libraries, which want to go in for digitizing their collection and making it available on internet. It's very well suited for countries like India, where there are many small libraries attached to colleges and other institutes ,which cannot afford to buy commercially available digital library software.

REFERENCES

Witten (I H) and Boddie (S). Greenstone Digital Library Istaller Guide. 2004; p. 1-30.

Witten (I H) and *et.al.* .Greenstone Digital Libray Users Guide. 2004. p. 1-68.

http://www.Greenstone org.

http://www.nzdl.org.

Chapter-6

CREATION OF THE SUBJECT GATEWAY OF LIS WEB RESOURCES USING GSDL: A PRACTICAL APPROACH

6.1 THROUGH GREENSTONE LIBRARIAN INTERFACE

Greenstone Librarian Interface (GLI) is the way through which user can build a new collection. GLI allows the user to select sets of documents, import or assign metadata and build them into a Greenstone collection.

It supports five basic steps.

i. Copy documents from computer file space, including existing collections, into a new collection. Any existing metadata remains "attached" to these documents.

Documents may also be gathered from the web through a built in mirroring function;

ii. Enriching the document by adding further metadata to individual documents or group of documents;

iii. Design the collection by determining its appearance and the access facilities that it will support;

iv. Built the collection using Greenstone; and

v. Preview the newly created collection, which have been installed in Greenstone Homepage as one of the regular collection.

The librarian interface allows to add what people call "external metadata" to document metadata that pertains to the document as a whole but document often used to be structured into setting and subsetting.

The librarian interface can be run in one of the four modes: librarian assistant, librarian, library system specialist and expert model control the level of details within the interface and can be changed through "preferences."

Launch the librarian interface under windows by selecting Greenstone Digital Library from the programme setting of short menu and choosing Greenstone Librarian Interface. To begin, one must either open an existing collection or short a new one.

6.1.1 Creating a New collection

To create a New Collection, open the 'File' menu and choose 'New'. Several fields need to be filled but one can change his/her value if need to.

'Title' in the text displayed at the top of the collection homepage. It can be of any length.

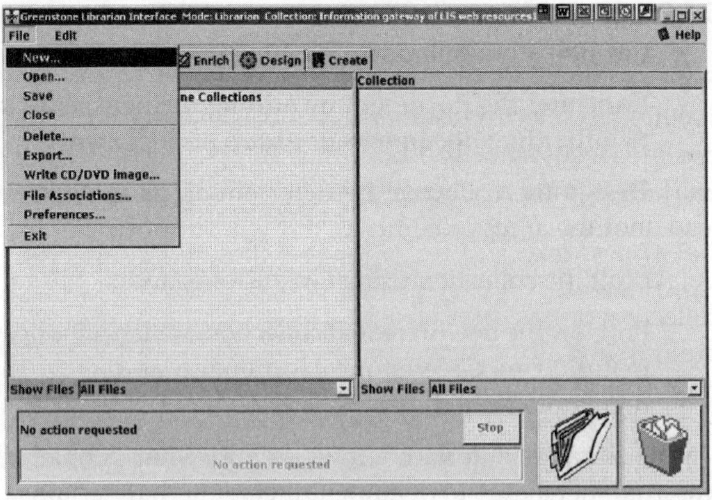

Fig. 20: Step-1 for create collection

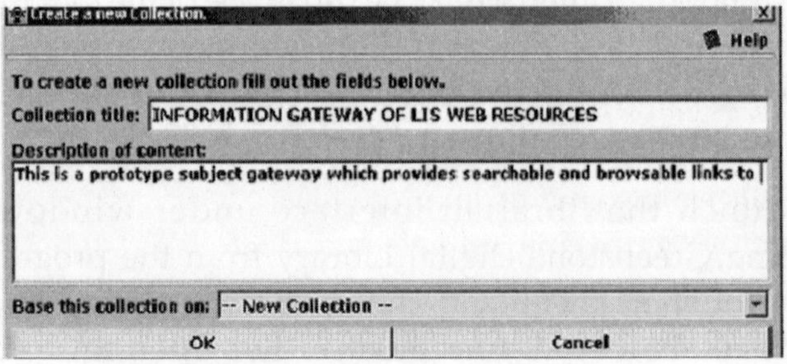

Fig. 21: Create collection view

"Description of Content" showed be desirable, in as many details as possible, what the collection is about. Use <Enter> key to break into paragraph.

Click 'OK' to create the new collection if you choose "new collection". You are prompted for the metadata sets to use in it. You can choose near than one metadata sets.

6.1.2 Saving the collection

Save your work by opening 'file' menu and choosing 'save', saving the collection is not the same as making it ready for use in Greenstone. The Librarian Interface protects one's work by saving it whenever one exists the programme or load another collections.

At this point user decides whether to base the new collection on the same structure as in existing collections or build externally a new kind of collection. In the present project, the creator named her collection as "subject Gateway of LIS Web Resources" and given the description about the collection like, what the collection has and how to search this collections etc.

6.1.3 Assembling the Source Material

After clicking the 'OK' button on the 'new collection' popup, the remaining part of the interface, which were grouped out before, became active. The 'Gather' panel by the eponymous tab near the top of figure (previous) is displayed initially. This allows the user to xexplore local file space and existing collection, gathering up selected documents for the new collection. This panel is divided into two sections, the left for browsing existing structures and the right for 'document in the collection'.

1. Navigating the existing file structure hierarchy, and the one being created, in the usual way.

i. Dragging an dropping files into new collection.

ii. Multiple selection of files.

iii. Dragging and dropping entire sub-hierarchies.

iv. Deleting document from the nascent collections.

v. Filtering the files that are visible, in both the local file system and the collection, based on predetermined groups or on standard file matching system.

vi. Invoking the appropriate programme to display the content of a selected file, by double clicking it.

Care is taken to deal appropriately with name clashes when files of the same name in different parts of the computer's directory structure are copied into the same folder of the collection.

From the home folder (system-04) all the document which were collected from various websites and gateways and stored in a folder has been taken into the new collection, named as Information Gateway of LIS Web Resources.

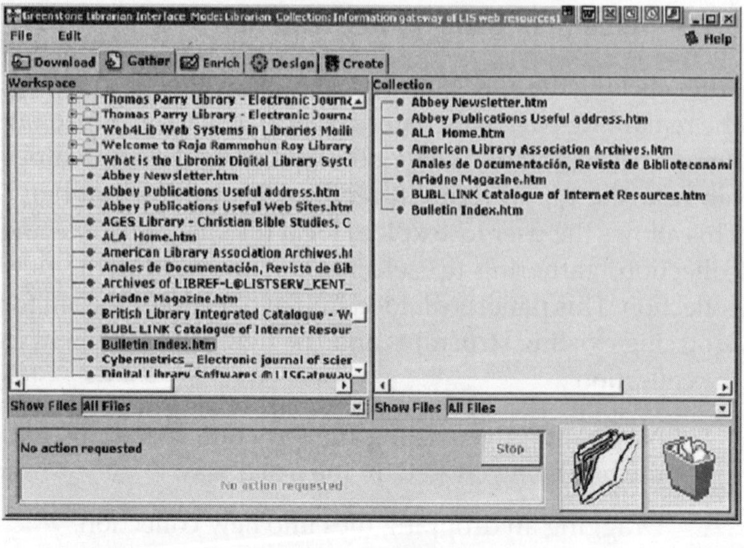

Fig. 22: The newly collected files from gather view.

6.2 ENRICHING THE DOCUMENT

The next phase of collection building is to enrich the

document by adding metadata. The enrich tab brings up a new panel of information. Figure.21 shows the document tree representing the collection on the left and on the right allows metadata to be added to individual documents or groups of documents.

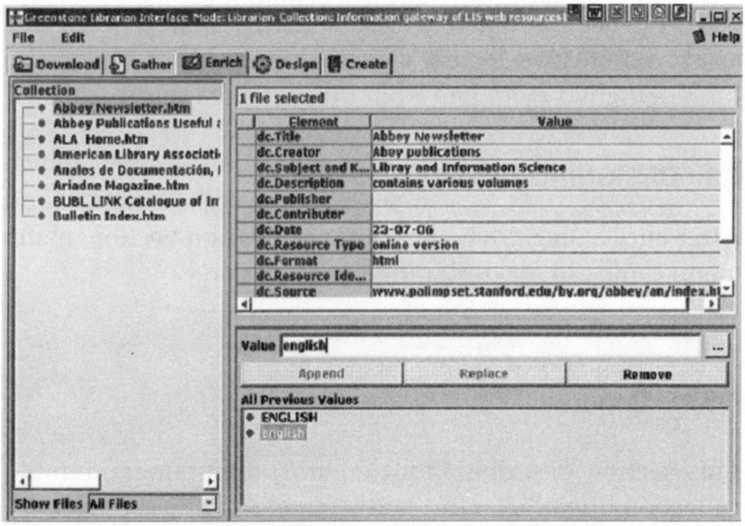

Fig. 23: Assigning metadata using enrich view.

Showing assign metadata using enrich view metadata value can also be assigned to folders, in just the same way.

Operation at this stage includes.

i. Assigning new and existing value to document;

ii. Assigning metadata to an individual document;

iii. Assigning metadata to a folder (this is inherited by all documents in the folder including thus in nested folders);

iv. Assigning hierarchical metadata, whose structure can be dynamically updated if required.

v. Editing and updating assigned metadata.

vi. Reviewing the metadata assigned to a selection of files and directories; and

vii. During the enrichment phase, or indeed at any other time, the user can choose to view all the metadata that has been assigned to documents in the collections. This is done by selecting a set of documents and choosing assigned metadata from the metadata sets menu.

6.3 DESIGNING THE COLLECTION

After enrich stage, when clicking on Design Section, a sub menu came out for designing the collection.

There are two stages in it, these are;

6.3.1 General

This section describe about creator, maintainers, e-mail, collection title or icon for 'home page' and about page.

6.3.2 Document Plugin

This section describes how to configure the document plugins, the collection uses. It explains how and what plugin to use, what parameter to pass to them, in what order they occur under "Design Section".

To add a plugin , select it using the "Select plugin to add" pull down list near the botton and then click "add plugin". A window appears entitled: Configuring arguments". Once you have configured the plugin, it is added to the end of the currently assigned plugins first.

To remove plugin select it from the list and click "Remove Plugin".

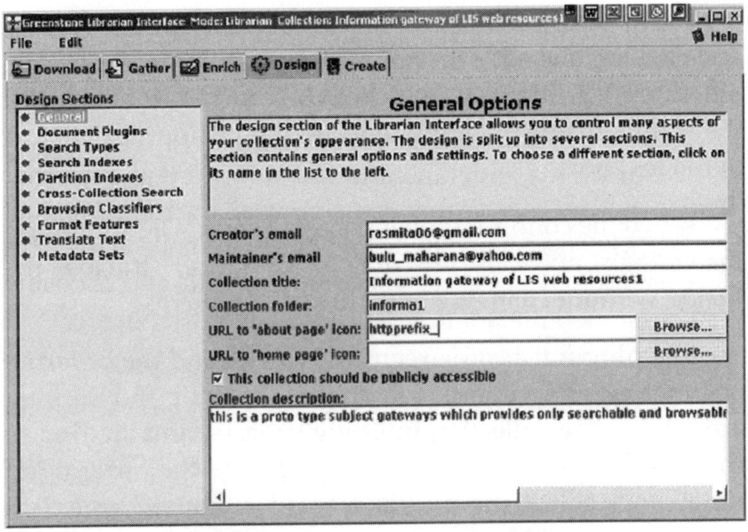

Fig. 24: Design view of general section.

Plugin are configured by providing arguments. To alter them select plug in from the list and "configure plug in". A "Configure Argument" dialog box appears.

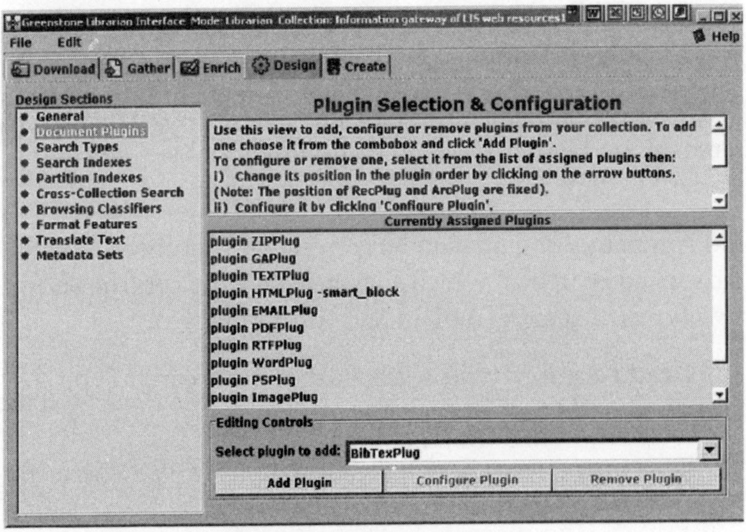

Fig. 25: The document Plugin

There are different kinds of control. Some are checkboxes and clicking one adds the appropriate options to the plugin, others are text strings with a check box and a text field. Click the box to enable the arguments then type appropriate text in the text box.

When the configuration is changed, click 'OK' to commit the changes and close the dialog, or "cancel" to close the dialog without changing any plug in arguments.

The plugin lists are executed in order and the ordering is sometimes important. Two plugins, Arcplug and Recplug are vital to the collection building process, and are find in the place at the end of the list. To change the ordering of other ones select the plugin wanted to move and click "move to top", "Move up" and "move down" or "move to buttons". The librarian interface does its best to determine what arguments plugin supports. However, there may be cases, where the user want to specify special arguments, and for this a text field called "custom argument" is provided.

6.3.3 Search Types

This section explains how to modify a new design feature in Greenstone Search types, which allows fielded searching, under "Design Section" click "Search Types".

After enterting on search types views, first check "Enable Advanced Searches" which activates the other control. Shows two types of search (i) plain and (iii) forma.

To add a search type, select it from the "Search Type" list and click "Add Search types".

To remove search types, select it from the currently assigned search types.

6.3.4 Search Indexes

Indexes specify what part of the collection are available. This section explains how to add and remove indexes, and set a default index. Under design section, click "Search Indexes".

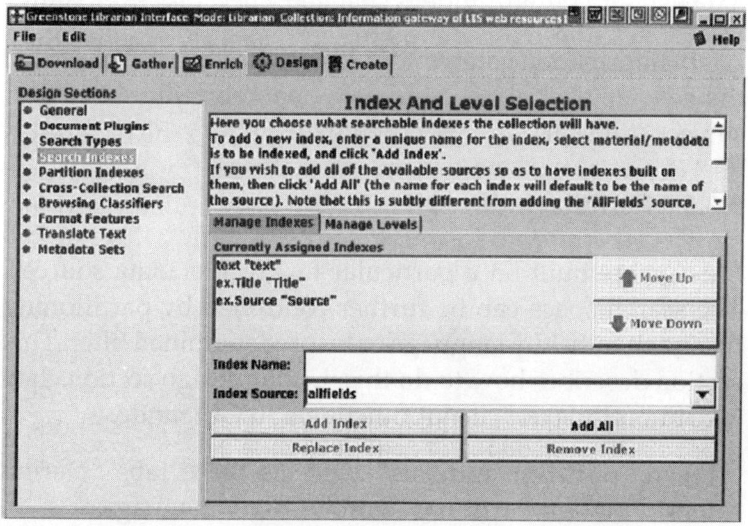

Fig. 26: Assigning index to the Collection view

To add an index type a name for it to be entered into the "index name" field. Select which of the possible information sources to index by clicking the checkboxes. The lists shows all the assigned metadata, choose it from the menu. Once these details are completed, "add index" become active. Click it to add the new indexes.

To remove an index, select it from the assigned indexes and click "Remove Index".

If advanced searching is enabled, the index control are different. Each index is based on just one data source. There is new pseudodata source "all fields" which provides searching across all specified indexes at once. Thus, indexes and level are added separately. Indexes are removed in the same way as above.

To create an index on all sources click the "Add all" button. The name of each index will default to the source name.

In Information gateway of LIS Web Resources Collection, the scholar has take n four fields namely, title, keyword, subject and year.

6.3.5 Partition Indexes

Indexes are built on a particular text or metadata sources. The search space can be further controlled by partitioning the index, either by language or by predetermined filter. This section describes how to do this. Under design section click "Partition Indexes", is not functional in GLI mode.

The "partition indexes" view as three tabs "Define filters", "Assign Partitions" and "Assign Languages".

6.3.5.1 Define Filter

Filter allows you to group together into a subcollections all document in an index for which metadata value matches a given pattern.

To create a filter, click the "Define Filters" tab and enter a name for new filter into the name the sub collection filter field. Next choose a document attribute to match against either a metadata element or the name of the file in question. Enter a regular expression to use during the matching. You are toggle between "including" documents that match the filter, or "Excluding" them. Finally, specify through using any of the standard PERL regular expression flags to use when matching. Finally click on "add filter" to add the filter to the "Defined sub collection filters" list.

6.3.5.2 Assign Partitions

Having defined a sub collection filter, use the "Assign Partitions" tab to build indexes for it. Select the desired filter from the "Defined sub collection filters" list, enter a name for the partitions in the "partition names" field and click "add partitions".

To remove a partition, select it from the list and click "Remove Partitions"

6.3.5.3 Assign Language

This section deals how to restrict search indexes to particular languages. This will be done through by generating a partition using the "Assign Languages" tab of the "Partition Indexes" view.

To add a new language to partition by, use the :Assign Languages" tab to build an index for it. Select the desired language from the "Languages to add" pull down list and click "Add Language"

6.3.6 Cross-Collection Searching

Greenstone can search across several different collection as though they were one. This is done by creating a "super collection" that comprises the individual collection. Under "Design Sections" click "Cross-Collection Search".

The cross-collection search view shows a checklist of available collections. The current collection is ticked and can not be deselected. To add another collection to be searched in parallel, click it in the list (Click again to remove it)

6.3.7 Classifiers

This section explains has to assign "classifiers" which are used for browsing to the collections Under "Design Selections", click "Browsing Classifiers".

To add a classifier, select it using the "Select Classifier to add" pull down list near the button and then click "Add specified classifier". A window appears entitled "Configuring Arguments", instructions for this dialogs are just the same as for analysis. Once you have configured the new classifier, it is added to the end of the "currently Assigned Classifier". To change the arguments a classifier, select it from the list and click "Configure Select Classifier, select it from the list and click "Configure selected classifier". The ordering of classifiers in the collections navigation bar is selected in their order here. To change it, select the classifier wanted to move and click "move to top". "move up", "move down" or "move to bottom".

The custom A-Z list classifier is a special classifier that builds an alphabetical selection list ("A-Z list") and allows to specify the letter ranges.

6.3.8 Format Features

Format commands control the structure and appearance of collections. One can apply a format command to any thing in the "Choose feature" pull down list, which include each classifier and a predefined list of feature when selecting a feature, there are two types of control. Some feature are simply enabled or disabled and this is controlled by check boxes. For these, there is a pull down list for selecting which part of the feature the string applies to, the text (HTML Strings) for entering and a selection of predefined "variables".

To add a new format command fill out the information as explained above and click "Add Format". To remove a format command, select it from the list, modify the setting and click "Replace Format".

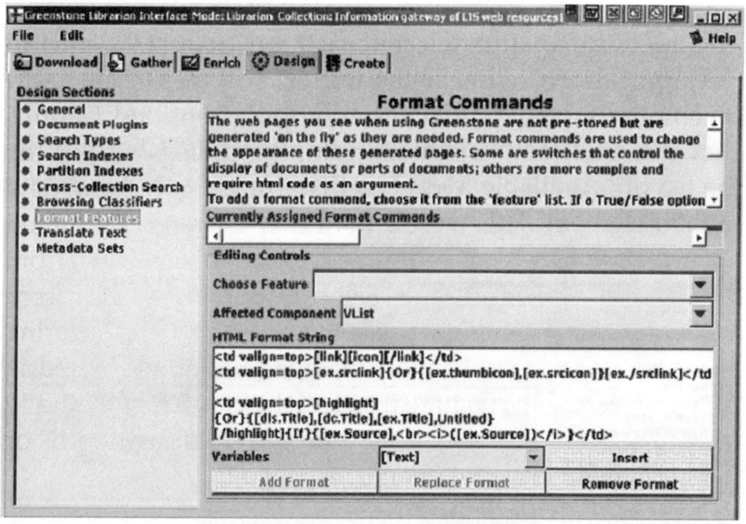

Fig. 27: Format Features of Greenstone Collection

6.3.9 Translate Text

This section describes the translation view, where one can define language specific text fragments for part of the collection interface. Under "Design Sections" Click "Translate Text".

First choose the entry from the "Features" list. The language specific strings associated with this feature appears below. Use the "Language of Translation" pull down list to select the target language, and type the translate text into the text area, referring to the "Initial Text Fragment" if necessary. Click "Add Translation" when finished.

In this project there was no need of any translation of text, because the text are already in English. So hence the scholar did not modify any sequence.

6.3.10 Metadata set

This section explains the metadata set review panel user "Design Section" click "metadata sets". This view used to review the metadata that the collection user, and that the elements that are available within each sets. Choose from the list of "Available Metadata Sets" in order to see details of their element. This view is read only.

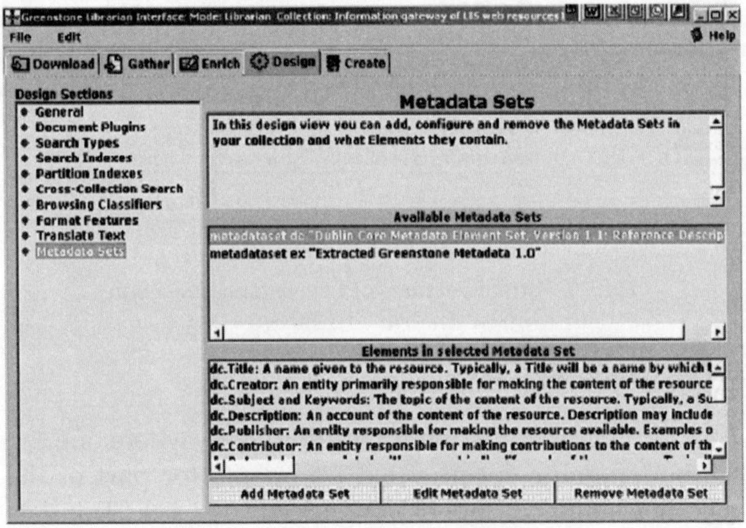

Fig. 28: The type of metadata

6.4 GETTING READY TO CREATE NEW COLLECTION

The create panel is used to construct a collection based on the document and assigned metadata.

The user observes the building process through a window that shows not only the text output generated by

Greenstone importing and index building scripts, but also progress bars that indicted the overall degree of completion of each script.

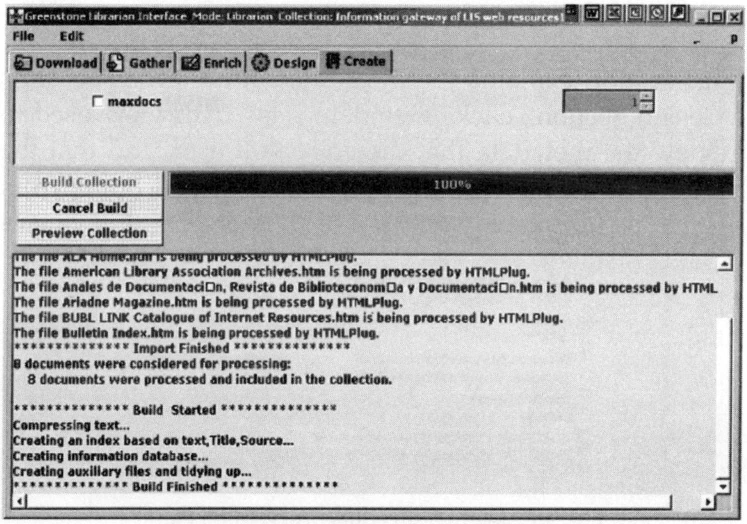

Fig. 29: Build Collection View.

When satisfied with the arguments, then click "Build collection". Greenstone continually points text that indicate progress and this is shown along with a more informative bar.

6.5 PREVIEWING THE COLLECTION

The 'Preview Collection' buttons is used to view the collection that has been built. Clicking this button launches a web browser showing the home page of the collection. In practice, Greenstone often shows up deficiencies in the collection design, or in the individual metadata values, and the user frequently returns to earlier stages to correct these. This button becomes active once the collection has been created.

The newly created collection will also have been installed on Greenstone Home page as one of the regular collections.

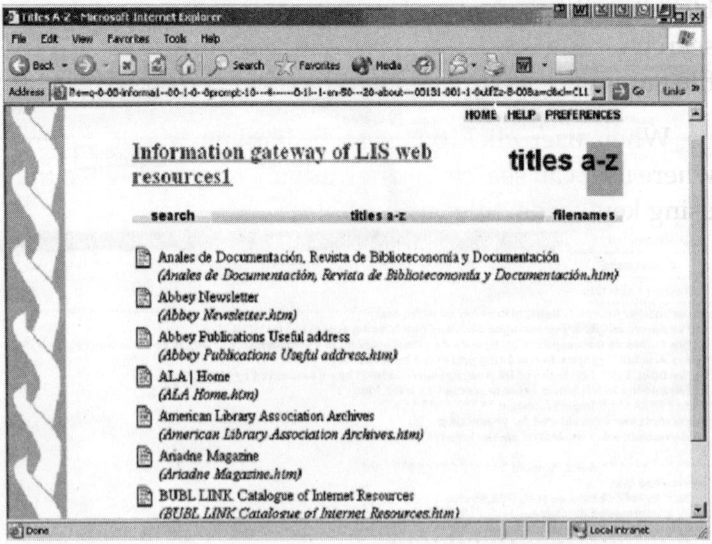

Fig. 30: Newly built collection (Home Page)

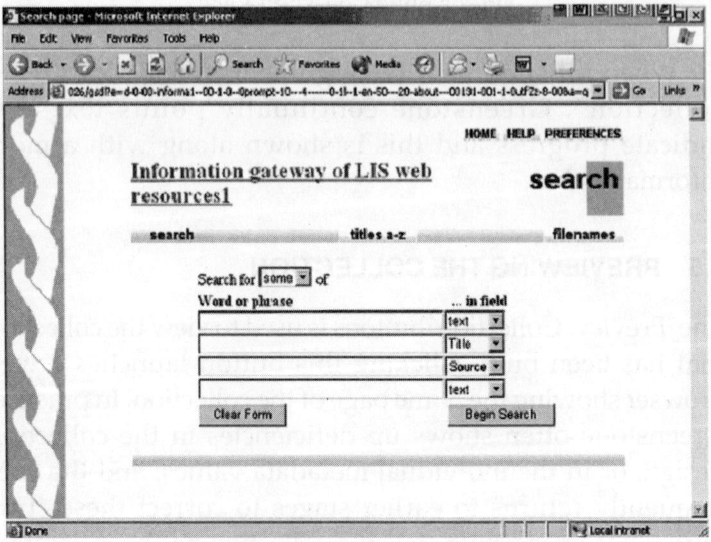

Fig. 31: The Search Page.

After the collection is ready, users can search through title, filenames or giving keyword in search box. This is the Home page of the collection. From this Home page, user can search other pages through the option like search, title a-z, file name etc.

When user click on search displays above figure.29, where user can search through advance searching technique using keywords, title, authors etc.

Chapter-7

OBSERVATIONS, SUGGESTIONS & CONCLUSION

Observations
Suggestions and Recommendations
Conclusion

7.1 OBSERVATIONS

In each and every project work, there must have certain observation. Hence, while doing the project work, the investigators observed the following facts.

- It is not possible to provide links to all types of LIS web resources through GSDL software, through some web pages has their own privacy policies.
- Through this project the usability of various web resources can be improved and the surfing time of the users will be saved.
- Building the collections for the Gateway can be more effectively and successfully done in an online environment.
- Practically it has been viewed and observed that the collection and links of various web resources such as

articles, databases, conference proceedings are easily and successfully browsed using given keyword facility.

- It is possible to browse directly all types of collections available in the Gateway in an online environment.
- Value added metadata description was made, which was available when the resources were at their original sources. As such it significantly enhances the searchability and browsability of the materials
- Multiple access could be possible from various terminal units in the department network, when the GSDL is made web enable.
- The operating modules of GSDL are very easy and user friendly.
- It is really very difficult to develop a full fledged subject Gateway with in a limited time.
- GSDL software has the potential to build and maintain the Gateway of Web resources but not with much more completeness as with the help of any other content management software and markup language.
- The GSDL software is much more effective for building digital collections successfully in the libraries and information centres.
- While referring to projects already been completed, it has been observed that, there is a continuous and mass research and development activities already in the process to update the GSDL Software.
- This project carries immensely practical value as it is the only project of its kind, provides a better opportunity for users to access different resources through the easy browsing and searching interface.

7.2 SUGGESTIONS & RECOMMENDATIONS FOR FURTHER STUDY

The present work essentially has an academic value. Though, the project has been completed with in a limited time frame. But the scholars recommend the further study can be taken up on the following directions

- Present Gateway Project is the accompanied with a limited number of web resources to keep pace with the limited time and effort, further more number and types of resources should be added into it.
- A systematic step should be taken for the regular updating if the links provided in it.
- A systematic step should be taken for web enabling the Gateway project so that the users can directly search all the websites to which links has been provided.
- A further step can be taken to make this project available on the web.
- This project will be immensely helpful, if the web resources will be selected according to the analysis of the user needs or with the recommendation about the most widely used URLs of the web resources.

7.3 CONCLUSION

Like any other fields, the resources in LIS subject domains are also increasing at a fast rate in all its forms from the printed to the electronic form. Now a days users are more reliant on web based resources due to their currency and authenticity, and multimedia features. But it is very difficult to get a required resources from the jungle of resources on the web though different resources are place at different resources are placed at different websites. Thus there is a need from organisational structure and an effective tools for retrieving them successfully. As a solution to this a number of subject gateways have been developed and a good number of such projects are under process, the existing project is also an initiation. Imitating the development of a subject gateway necessitates an appropriate software and an open source software is always suggested as suitable for developing such a mechanism. Among a number of open source software (GSDL) seems to an effective one due to its multilingual, multiplatform and multimedia enabled features.

The present work has immense practical value and another addition to the number of LIS gateway initiatives. However, it needs sustain implementation such as web-enabling, extension of categories, regular updating of the existing category of web resources will prove it to be a highly useful tool for LIS Professionals, students, researchers etc.

BIBLIOGRAPHY

Accanoor (Kalyani). An overview of the Subject Gateway: Material Science. Caliber. 2003. Feb. 13-15; Ahmedabad; p. 13-15.

Arora (Jagdish). Web Based Digital Resources and Services: Trends and Innovations. Caliber. 2001. Feb. 15-16; Pune; p. 209.

Choudhry (Om Kumari). Information Gateway of Social Science in India. Caliber. 2003. Feb. 13-15; Ahmedabad; p. 48-69.

Das (Pankaj Kumar). Subject Gateways: The Clever Way to Information. Caliber. 2001. Feb. 15-16; Pune; p. 220-224.

Howarth (Lynnec). Metadata Schemas for Subject Gateways. 69th IFLA General Conference and Council. 2003. Aug. 1-9; p. 78-80.

Krishnamurthy (M). Subject Gateways to Library and Information Science on the NET: An Experience. ILA Seminar Papers. 2003; p. 341-345.

Palace (Emma). International Collaboration on Internet Subject Gateways. IFLA Journal. Vol. 26(1). 2000; p. 52-56.

Raza (MM) and EqbaL (M). Subject Gateways: Its Need and Development Isssues. SIS 2004; p. 84-89.

Sahoo (BB) and rao (I K. Ravichandra). Planning & Designing of Digital Library. IASLIC National Seminar, (xx); Patiala; 2002; p. 1-8.

Shivalngaiah (D) and manjunatha (K). Digital Library in the Networked World. Electronic Libraries; P. Sadasiva-murthy Festschrift. 2002. May; p. 50-55.

Witten (I H) and boddie (S). Greenstone Digital Library Installer Guide. 2004; p. 1-30.

Witten (I H) and et.al. Greenstone Digital Library User's Guide. 2004; p. 1-68.

WEBLIOGRAPHY

Ariadne Issue 25.2004. Retrieved on 31st May, 2006 from (http://www.ariadene.ac.uk)

Australian Gateways. Retrieved on 25th May,2006 from (http://www.nla_gov.au)

BUBL. Retrieved on 10th July, 2006 from (http://www. bubl.ac.uk)

Bibliotech. Retrieved on 10th July ,2006 from (http://www.infolibrarian.com)

Canadian Library Gateway. Retrieved on (Http://www.collectionscanada.ca/index.html)

Information City. Retrieved on 20th July, 2006 from (http://www.information city.com)

Information Gateways Handbook. Browsed on 20th June from (http://www.desire.org)

ILL Web. Downloaded on 20th July, 2006 from (http://www.illweb.org)

Internet Public Library. Retrieved on (http://www.ipl.org)

Greenstone Digital Library. Retrieved on 20th June, 2006 from (http://www.greenstone.org)

Librarian Internet Index. Retrieved on 23rd July, 2006 from (http://www. lii.org)

Library World. Retrieved on 20th July, 2006 from (http://www.libraryworld.co.uk)

New Zealand Digital Library Project. Visited on 11th May, 2006 from (http://www.nzdl.org)

Online Megazine. November 2002. Retrieved on 22th May, 2006 from (http://www.onlineinc.com/onlinemag/ol2000/oleary//html)

Tools for information retrieval on the Internet retrieved on 29th April,2006 from (http://www.geocity.com)

Virtual Library. Visited on 23rd July, 2006 from (http://www. vlib.org)

GLOSSARY

Autoconf	A Unix programmes used to configure the Greenstone Software installation package to suit your system
Auto run	Windows feature that starts a programme automatically whenever a CD-ROM is inserted.
BookMark	Local folder on the browser which permits the users to add an e-address of an document for future references as a local file.
Boolean Query	Query to an information retrieval system that may contain AND, OR, NOT.
Browsing	Accessing a collection by scanning and organised list of metadata values associated with the documents (such as author, title, date and keywords)
Buildcol.pl	Greenstone Programme used to build the collection
Building	The process of creating indexing and browsing structures that are used to access a collection.
Client	A programme that request a service of another computer or programme. *e.g.*, to download a file from a remote computer

C++	Programming language in which the majority of Greenstone Software is written
CGI	Stands for Common Gateway Interface, is a scheme that allows users to active programmes on the host computer by clicking on web pages
CGI Script	Code associated with a button, menu, or link on a web page that specifies what the host computer is to do when it is clicked.
CGI-bin	Directory in which CGI scripts are stored.
Classified	Greenstone Core module that examines document metadata to forms an index for browsing
Collection	A set of documents that are brought together under a uniform searching and browsing interface.
Collection Configuration file	File that specifies how a collection is to be imported and built, what index and language interfaces are to be provided etc.
Collection Server	Programme responsible for providing access to a collection when it is been used.
Demo Collection	A subset of the Humanities Development Library, distributed with the Greenstone Software and used for illustration in the tutorial.
Digital Library	Collection of Digital Object (text, audio, video) along with method for access and retrieval and for selection, organisation, and maintenance
Doublin Core	A standard way of describing metadata.
FTP	File Transfer Protocol consist of standard set up commands for file downing and uploading. It is used to transfer file between network and computers
Firstcgi	Facility that allows cgiscrift to remains continuous active so that they do not have to be restarted from scratch every time they are invoked

Format string	A string that specifies how documents and other listings are to be displayed in Greenstone
GDBM	GNU Database manager, a programme used in the Greenstone software to store metadata for each document
GML	Greenstone Markup Language, an XML compliant format used for storing document internally
GNU License	Software License that permits users to copy and distribute computer programme freely and modify them so long as all modifications are made publicly available
%GSDL	Operating System variable that represents the top level
HOME%	directory in these all Greenstone programmes and collections are stored.
%GSDL OS%	Operating System variables that represents the operating system currently being used
Hash file	Green stone programme use at import or built time to generate the OID of each document
HTML	Hypertext Markup Language, the language in which web documents are written
Deliverable	Output
Import.Pl	Greenstone Programme used to import documents
Importing	Process of bringing collections of documents into the Greenstone system
Index	Information structure that is used for searching and browsing a collection
Installed shield	Windows programme used by a CD-ROMs, that allows a system to be installed from a CD-ROM
http	Hypertext transport protocol. It is the basis for www and an import network layer protocol

Homepage	A special document that is intended to be viewed first, one that contains introductory information and/or, a master menu of documents within that collection. This is generally associated with a particular site, person or named collection
Main configuration file	File that contains specifications common to all collection served by this side
Metadata	Descriptive data that is data about data such author, title, date, keywords and so on, that is associated with a document or document collection
MG	Managing Gigabyte, a programme used by the greenstone system for fulltext indexing that incorporate compression techniques.
MG Build	MG programme for building a compressed fulltext index.
Mgquery	Mg Programme for queering a compressed full text index
Mirror site	Mirror site is the site like the repository of resources which can be located by other member or partner sites.e.g.the resources available at INDEST can be located by its members from different places.
Mkcol.Pl	Greenstone that creates and initializes the directory structure for a new collection
New Zealand Digital Library Project	Research Project in computer science department at the university of waikato, New Zealand that created the Greenstone software
OID	Object Identifier is a unique identification code associated with a document
OSS	Open source software is a software whose source code is associated with a document.
Perl	Programming Language used for many of the text processing operations that occurred during the building process

Plugin	Code module for handling documents of different formats used during the importing and building process.
Ping	Message sent to a system to determine whether it is running or not
Protocol	A set of convention by which a Greenstone receptionist communicates with a collection server
Ranked query	Natural language query to a information retrieval system for which the document that match the query are stored in order of relevance.
Receptionist	Programme that organises the Greenstone User Interface
RTF	Rich text format, a standard format for interchange of text document
Search Engine	Search Engine is a internet tool that index other pages, e.g-Google
Searching	Accessing a collection through a full text search of its content (or parts of content, such as section, titles)
Server	Is a programme or computer that provides service to other computers
Setup.bat, setup.sh, setup.csh	Script used to setup your environment to recognise the greenstone software.
Site configu-ration file	File that contains specification used to con-figure the greenstone. it is the software for the site on which it is installed.
Stemming	Stripping ending of a query term to make it more general.
Tag	A tag is a unit of markup, a set of symbols defined in HTML to have special meaning. Tag starts and ends with angle brackets followed by a keyword, *e.g.*<img>.
Txt2db	Greenstone programme used at build time to create the GDBM database.

Unicode	Standard scheme for representing the character of sets used in the words language.
UNU	The United Nations University also used to refer to a Greenstone collection created for that organisation.
URL	Uniform Resource Locator is used by WWW to represent hypermedia links and links to network services within HTML documents.
VPN	Virtual Private Network.It builds a top private network.Its host within the private network,the use of encryption and tunnelling to talk other hosts
Web Server	Standard programme that computers used to make information accessible over the world wide web.
Web page	Is a special type of file and hypermedia document written in HTML.
Website	The location where the webpages are stored.
XML	Extended Markup Language is a standard format for structured documents and data on the web (The Greenstone Markup Language is an XML compliant format.
Z39.50	An information retrieval protocol and standard.

Appendix-I

OPEN SOURCE SOFTWARE FOR LIBRARIES

Name of the software	Web address
Avanti, An open source library computing system	http://www.avantilibrary systems.com/
Ganesha digital library	http://www.gdl.itb.al.id
Greenstone Digital Library Software	http://www.greeenstone. org.
Ivia open source virtual library system	http://infomine.ucr.edu/ ivia/ivia.php
Jake, a metadata collective for e-journals	http://jake.med.yale.edu/
Koha, open source library system	http://www.koha.org/
Leaming Access ILS	http://www.leamingaccess. gaccess.org/website/tele chdev/ils.pp
My Library	http://dewey.library.nd. edu/my-library/
Open OPAC	http://www.bl.fcen.ubar/ openopac.php

Name of the software	Web address
Open Source Digital Library System	http://www.library.arizona.edu/users/ifrumkin/osdls/about.html/
Php mybibli	http://phpmybibli.sourceforge.net
Research guide	http://researchguide.sourceforge.net/
Virtual library: Open source information broker	http://vu.wu.wien.ac.at/virlib/

Appendix-II

IMPORTANT SUBJECT GATEWAYS

Name	*Coverage*	*Url*
ADAM	Art, Design, Architecture and Media Resources	http://www.adam.ac.uk
EELS	Engineering Resources	http://www.eels.lub.lu.se
EEVL	Engineering	http://www.eevl.ac.edn
NBW	Internet Resources intended to Dutch Academic Community	http://www.konbib.nl
OMNI	Medicine	http://www.omni.ac.uk
RUDI	Multimedia Resource for research and teaching in urban design	http://www.rudi.verts.ac.uk
SOSIG	Social Science	http://www.sosig.ac.uk

Name	*Coverage*	*Url*
Infolib-rarian.com	Library & Information Science	http://www.infolibrarian.com
LIS Gat-eway.com	Library & Information Science	http://www.lisgateway.com
BUBL	All disciplines	http://www.bubl.ac.uk
Acade-micinfo	Education and Research	http://www.academicinfo.com

INDEX